The Survivability of Catholic Schools

The Survivability of Catholic Schools

Vigor, Anemia, and a Diffident Flock

Michael P. Caruso, SJ

ROWMAN & LITTLEFIELD
Lanham • Boulder • New York • London

Published by Rowman & Littlefield
An imprint of The Rowman & Littlefield Publishing Group, Inc.
4501 Forbes Boulevard, Suite 200, Lanham, Maryland 20706
www.rowman.com

86-90 Paul Street, London EC2A 4NE

Copyright © 2022 by Michael P. Caruso

All rights reserved. No part of this book may be reproduced in any form or by any electronic or mechanical means, including information storage and retrieval systems, without written permission from the publisher, except by a reviewer who may quote passages in a review.

British Library Cataloguing in Publication Information Available

Library of Congress Cataloging-in-Publication Data

Names: Caruso, Michael P., author.
  Title: The survivability of Catholic schools : vigor, anemia, and a diffident flock / Michael P. Caruso.
  Description: Lanham, Maryland : Rowman & Littlefield, 2022. | Includes bibliographical references. | Summary: "This book guides readers through the hard-won legacy of Catholic schools in the United States to become the largest private school system in the country"-- Provided by publisher.
  Identifiers: LCCN 2022032538 (print) | LCCN 2022032539 (ebook) | ISBN 9781475867923 (hardback) | ISBN 9781475867930 (paperback) | ISBN 9781475867947 (epub)
  Subjects: LCSH: Catholic schools--United States. | Catholic Church--Education--United States.
  Classification: LCC LC501 .C284 2022 (print) | LCC LC501 (ebook) | DDC 371.071/273--dc23/eng/20220821
  LC record available at https://lccn.loc.gov/2022032538
  LC ebook record available at https://lccn.loc.gov/2022032539

Praise Page

"A decade after publishing *When the Sisters Said Farewell*, Fr. Michael Caruso revisits the current reality of Catholic schools in American society. With his extensive leadership experience, insightful understanding of the relevant issues, and a devout faith in Jesus Christ, Fr. Caruso explores critical topics facing our Catholic schools and provides practical advice on holding fast to the mission and foundation that has served our schools well for nearly two centuries."—Anthony de Nicola, Chairman at Welsh, Carson, Anderson & Stowe, New York. Along with his wife Christie, they are active leaders in supporting Catholic schools.

"Father Caruso, himself a scholar and seasoned educator, writes with 'tough love' about our 'pearl of great price,' our Catholic schools. If we want to replace the ominous interrogation mark after 'Catholic Schools?' with a bold exclamation mark, this book sure helps."—Timothy Cardinal Dolan, PhD, DD, Archbishop of New York

"Father Caruso blends experience and anecdotes to paint a picture of the challenges in Catholic education today. Everyone who has a role in Catholic education will find his frank commentary thought-provoking and useful for envisioning the future of Catholic schools."—Bishop Michael McGovern, Diocese of Belleville

"This is an exceedingly timely book. Fr. Michael Caruso, who has previously written so well on the contributions of Catholic schools to American culture, once again reminds us of the nation's amazing, historic, Catholic school system—especially how it has succeeded in keeping its students strongly connected to the principles by which our nation stands 'undivided.' With this monograph, however, he leads us further. Fully aware of the ramifications of the dangerous secularizing trends that plague today's public schools, he encourages readers to once again take up the arduous challenge of returning to the classic standards of providing an education based on the original standards of the American public school system. This is why his book is such an absolutely essential guide for anyone who grapples with finding innovative ways to ensure a system that replicates what has worked so well these past two centuries. Our future as a free nation depends upon the part the Catholic Church plays in fulfilling these dreams of our ancestors. As a published historian on the contributions of Catholic men and women to the development of American society within a 'free' American society and as a Catholic educator—I am now Professor Emerita of Holy Apostles College and Seminary, Cromwell, CT—I am delighted that Fr Caruso has spoken for so many of us and commend him for offering us strong suggestions for future solutions. Above all, I thank him for reminding us that we are being asked, as Church, to do what public schools are now failing to do. For all those who care about a return to grounded and basic education for all, this is a must-read book."—Sister Dolores Liptak, RSM, PhD

"One piece of advice commonly given to students writing papers and authors of academic articles alike is to tell the readers what you are going to say, do it, and then tell them again at the end what you have said. In this well-crafted and impassioned book, Fr. Caruso has clearly taken this advice, providing the reader with an immensely useful overview of Catholic schools at this pivotal time. The voice of a seasoned administrator and gifted teacher who is also a distinguished historian of US Catholic schools speaks in these pages. The serious questions facing US Catholic education are aired, the author's 'warts and all' approach showing his deep familiarity with and love for his topic. This book is however about more than education. Catholic schools in the US have played an unusually large role in evangelization and building community, integrating immigrants into the mainstream of public life, and lifting people out of poverty. So, the current shifts and challenges in Catholic education both reflect and shape the whole of the US Church—and indeed have significant implications for US public life as a whole. Teachers, parents, administrators, pastors, trustees and donors, professors of education and bishops—and not a few publicly elected officials—should all read this powerful book."—Fr. Dorian Llywelyn SJ, President, Institute for Advanced Catholic Studies at the University of Southern California

Contents

Praise Page	v
Acknowledgements	ix
Introduction	xiii
Chapter 1: How We Got to This Point with Catholic Schools: Background	1
Chapter 2: "I Thought that This Was Supposed to Be a Catholic School?" (Parents and Mission)	17
Chapter 3: "We Hire for Mission and We Fire for Mission": Easier Said than Done!	33
Chapter 4: Religious Communities: Absentee Landlords	49
Chapter 5: Athletics: The Gift that Keeps Scoring!	63
Chapter 6: Technology: Its Joys and Woes!	77
Chapter 7: Liturgy and Service Can Moderate Technology	87
Chapter 8: Who Is Going to Pay What It Costs?	93
Conclusion	111
Bibliography	117
About the Author	121

Acknowledgements

This book got a start as I was ending a ten-year appointment as President of Saint Ignatius College Prep in Chicago and the first tsunami of Covid-19 was about to sweep around the globe. I distinctly remember walking through the dining room of our school in mid-March of 2020 when a senior girl beckoned me to her table. With great excitement and anticipation, she asked if the school would be taking a two-week break to let the virus work its way through society, as the news media was anticipating. I told her that we were watching the situation and would do what was prudent for safety. Little did she know, that was going to be her last full week at the school for in-class instruction.

Prom was canceled, though another dance was held a year later. There was no formal commencement ceremony, but faculty and administrators delivered diplomas and a box of graduation swag to each household. Another event was held at Navy Pier for the class in Spring of 2021, but it was all a peculiar ending for a fine class of young people.

June of 2020 was the conclusion of our Sesquicentennial Anniversary. We were to have a Mass at Holy Name Cathedral with Cardinal Cupich followed by a festive evening at Navy Pier. Alumni Bob Newhart and John Mulaney were to be the hosts of the program, joined by a longtime friend of the school, comedian George Wendt, who we were going to surprise with an honorary diploma that night. All of it was cancelled. I had been granted a year's sabbatical but my plans to serve as a chaplain at Lourdes and to do some traveling were all thwarted, like the best-laid plans of many people, but Plan B did emerge.

Cardinal Dolan told me that I should come to New York where I could be bored there instead of Chicago, but it was hardly boring. I am grateful for the hospitality and encouragement of his Eminence and his staff. Msgr. Joseph LaMorte, Fr. Stephen Ries, Ann Bave, Demaris Rosario, Antoine and Pickle Bouterin all welcomed me and provided an enjoyable setting to begin the book. During my time in New York, I was made an Honorary Citizen of Staten Island, aka the Pearl of the Atlantic, thanks to the friendship of pastors

Fr. James Ferriera and Fr. Freddy Patiño, at whose parishes I delivered Lenten Missions. Those fall months passed quickly and most enjoyably, as I tried to awaken the Writing Muses for this book.

I did not want another Chicago winter, so our community at Jesuit High School Tampa welcomed me. Jesuit Fathers Richard Hermes, Angel Rivera Fals, Joe Vanderholt, Paul Deutsch, and Giovanni Diaz-Jimenez were wonderful companions through the winter and early spring. I especially enjoyed seeing this remarkable flagship Jesuit institution and was struck by the exuberant spiritual life that infuses the school's culture. I am grateful for their hospitality and fraternal support.

As I considered the content of the book, I tried to think about what I had seen and learned from my experience as a university professor and administrator. The publisher was adamant that they did not seek a researched project; they wanted my perspective, such as it is. There is no shortage of fine books and articles about the history and current successes of Catholic schools. The excellent work of the schools, shown in test scores, demonstrates the effectiveness of the schools. The heroic labors among the poor are documented and told in diocesan papers as well as celebrated by the secular press. So, I wanted to offer something a bit different about the unseen challenges that the schools and their leaders face.

I am grateful for my ten years of leadership at Saint Ignatius College Prep. During those years, I enjoyed the collegial labors with Dr. Kathy Karl, Greg Gleason, Brianna Latko, Fr. Lukas Laniauskas, SJ, and John Chandler, who succeeded me as president. Those years provided wonderful opportunities to work with our board at the school and to serve on the Archdiocesan School Board of Chicago. Our schools are blessed with a richness of expertise in board members. The faculty and staff had among them some amazing superstars.

One of the more astonishing developments was welcoming the Dominican Sisters of Mary, Mother of the Eucharist, from Ann Arbor to teach at the school. I was particularly delighted that our students and families would get to know women religious even as our Jesuit numbers at the school were usually low. The sisters who joined us over the years brought their evangelizing spirit of joy and unwavering dedication to many disciplines. We usually had four sisters, but as I told Mother Assumpta Long and Sister Joseph Andrew at the Motherhouse, we would love to welcome more of the sisters. Thank you, Mother Assumpta and all the sisters!

While on sabbatical, I was in discernment with Father Thomas Greene, SJ, my provincial, about my next assignment. Among several possible opportunities, it was determined that I would return to province and begin working at Saint Louis University. I was welcomed by the Dean, Gary Ritter, and the faculty there to work in the Leadership Department and especially with aspiring

Catholic school administrators. That year allowed me to focus on getting this book finished and getting it to press. However, as a Jesuit, we must always be available for missioning and transitions.

Though my time at Saint Louis University was brief, I am grateful to the university for the opportunity to contribute to the mission. While in St. Louis, I lived at Jesuit Hall, which must be one of the largest communities in the nation with about seventy Jesuits living here. It is home to one of the province's infirmaries and retirement homes. During Covid, all the Jesuits who worked at the university were moved to different places. I am grateful to Father Phil Steele, SJ, our rector, who welcomed me, and the many men who offered a supportive and friendly home.

Upon arriving in St. Louis, I was invited to join the board at Saint Louis University High School. It was good to be connected with another great Jesuit High School. As life would have it, I was asked to join the leadership team there in the summer of 2022, and that is my new assignment as Vice President of Mission, Operations, and Planning.

The first person who comes to mind whenever I think about this project is my editor from Rowman and Littlefield, Tom Koerner. He must be given credit (or blame!) for prompting me to write this reflection on Catholic schools and cheerleading the project all along the way. Readers will likely have different views on the topics I propose, which is healthy for dialogue.

Ann Carey and Sister Dolores Liptak, RSM, not only offered comments for the book, but they also went above and beyond the call of duty by offering critical suggestions for the content and structure of the book. I am grateful for their generous gift of time and expertise.

Jim and Molly Perry are great advocates of Catholic schools, serving on various boards and passing along the experience to their own children. Jim has been active in the Archdiocese of Chicago and a leader in the School Choice movement in Illinois; I am grateful for their friendship and support of this project.

Tony de Nicola and his wife Christie have been among the great crusaders for Catholic schools in the New York area and nationwide. School leaders are blessed to have allies like the de Nicolas supporting them in so many ways.

Bishop Michael McGovern of the Diocese of Belleville, Illinois, is a strong advocate and supporter of Catholic schools and a good friend. I am grateful for his encouragement with this project and for being a neighbor in the St. Louis metropolitan area.

Fr. Dorian Llywelyn, SJ, is currently the President of the Institute for Advanced Catholic Studies at the University of Southern California. He is a well-regarded theologian with an international reputation and following. While able to converse on some of the most erudite topics, he also has both feet planted on the ground and is a great champion of Catholic schools as a means of passing along our faith. He has that enviable capacity to present complex theological concepts to everyone from know-it-alls in the "Jesuit Rec Room" to the First Communion candidates—and all done with good humor and a practical spirituality. I am grateful for his quick response to support this book.

Msgr. James Vlaun is an amazingly gifted priest and leader that everyone should get to know and can know through the Catholic Faith Network. If you are not familiar with the network and its programming, download the app and start watching. Do not miss his Real Food cooking programs that are on the app. However, in all fairness, plan to dash to the nearest Italian market or restaurant as soon as you have watched because it will trigger an appetite! Thank you Msgr. Vlaun for your kind words and gift of friendship over the years.

Pope Benedict XVI, speaking to the Clergy of Rome on May 13, 2005, offered a grounding insight that is most appropriate for the core mission of Catholic schools:

> If we have found the Lord and if he is the light and joy of our lives, are we sure that for someone else who has not found Christ he is not lacking something essential and that it is our duty to offer him this essential reality? . . . If we are convinced and we have experienced the fact that without Christ life is incomplete, is missing a reality, the fundamental reality, we must also be convinced that we do harm to no one if we show them Christ and we offer them in this way too the possibility to discover, the joy of having discovered life.

Ad Maiorem Dei Gloriam et Beatae Mariae Virgine Honore

Introduction

This book is an attempt to pull back the curtain on the inner workings of Catholic schools in the United States and to identify some of the challenges that the schools and their leaders are facing. There is no shortage of glowing reports about the success of Catholic education and generally these are accurate. During the COVID pandemic, government schools, more commonly known as public schools, were quick to send children home for working parents to figure out what might be next, while Catholic schools found ways to keep children engaged both virtually and in person. There is no question or lack of information about the force for good that Catholic schools are for society and the nation, but it comes at a great cost.

Throughout this book the term *government schools* will be used when speaking of public schools, because they derive their funding from and are managed solely by local, state, and to some degree, the federal government, elected and appointed officials. Whereas Catholic schools, both parochial and private, are chiefly governed and financed through a parish, a diocese, a religious order, and/or a board that oversees the school in concert with state requirements.

The sudden disappearance of a quality workforce that worked for next to nothing for decades disappeared long ago when teaching orders of sisters, brothers, and priests withdrew from schools to work in other ministries or due to their own march towards the endangered species list or extinction. It would take the Church decades to fill these shoes, but excellent lay women and men stepped forward. However, paying a living salary with meaningful benefits was not easily provided.

Sufficient finances remain an important driver for the success of Catholic schools. Good will and generosity are also essential ingredients but without the cash flow to run the schools, the project is in peril. Walking hand in hand with the fiscal realities are the demographics of where people live and how much appetite there is for a Catholic school education.

It is no secret that the Church is in a challenging period in making the teachings of Jesus Christ known and loved. Even young graduates who have the benefit of twelve or thirteen years of Catholic education are frequently liberating themselves from church membership to join the growing number of Nones, i.e., those who identify with no religious tradition, or with the Do-It-Yourself crowd of "I'm spiritual, but not religious."

One must wonder with the two years (2020–2022) of unprecedented upheaval caused by Covid and the frightening prospects of the savage war unleashed on the Ukraine, if a Spiritual Awakening might be in the near future. Humanity's propensity for thinking it can do things as well or better than God begins in the Garden of Eden and runs forward through the Bible and all recorded history. Such an awakening might serve as a catalyst for a renewed appreciation for a life of faith and the Catholic schools that cultivate it.

In the meantime, this book will share some of the thornier issues and challenges that are swirling in the Catholic schools across the nation. A hope for this excursus is that stakeholders will grow in their appreciation for the unseen labors of school leaders and those responsible for their success. There are many elephants dancing in the sacristy, school, and chancery offices that need to be addressed forthrightly.

In 1976, the entertainer Pearl Bailey wrote a book entitled *Hurry Up, America, and Spit*. It is a collection of her musings about the country getting its mission better organized and better utilizing its best resources, its people. Perhaps that title speaks to many people when things seem to go crazy in Catholic schools. If Catholic schools try to be all things to all people, where exactly are faithful, believing Catholics supposed to send their children? These schools should be communities of faith, hope, and love based on the teachings of Jesus and His Church. When these get compromised, trouble will certainly follow. This is a snapshot of the chapters:

Chapter 1: How We Got to This Point with Catholic Schools: Background—This chapter provides the reader with an abridged history of Catholic schools in the United States. This should be a useful orientation to the current realities that are described in the book. By no means is it meant to be an exhaustive history of the schools as there are other fine resources that have been written for that purpose.

Chapter 2: "I Thought that This Was Supposed to Be a Catholic School?" (Parents and Mission)—That quote is always invoked when a student gets into serious trouble and is asked to leave a school. Working with parents is challenging! A school's relationship is often described in its most positive way as a partnership, but sometimes school leaders are treated like the barista fulfilling a complicated order of coffee. Parents sacrifice and pay a good deal of money for a Catholic education, so it is not entirely unreasonable that they have high expectations of the leadership, but sometimes it crosses a line.

Chapter 3: "We Hire for Mission and We Fire for Mission": Easier Said than Done!—This title is a catch phrase one often hears in Leadership Classes and at big meetings for Catholic school leaders. Hiring is the simple part but dismissing problem employees is quite another. The court of public opinion is quick to crucify school leaders who make mission-based employment decisions. This chapter will explain what happens when an adult is dismissed or not renewed.

Chapter 4: Religious Communities: Absentee Landlords—Many religious communities have a passion for opening new schools like the Cristo Rey model, but those communities have no one to send and of what few recruits are entering religious life, very few want to work in schools; many want to serve in boutique ministries. Secondary school governance usually has a two-tiered board, or a membership requirement, that gives a simple majority veto power of the sponsoring community in either structure. The orders think by teaching their mottos, catch phrases, spiritual traditions, and information about their founder; it is sufficient to keep the charism vibrant, but is this really working or a case of the Emperor's New Clothes, i.e., seeing what one wants to see?

Chapter 5: Athletics: The Gift that Keeps Scoring!—Probably three-quarters of students in Catholic elementary and secondary schools participate in sports. There is no question that the field, the swimming pool, and the gym are significant classrooms where important lifelong lessons are learned, and friendships are forged. In secondary schools, the poor Athletic Director has one of the worst jobs in the school; in elementary schools this challenge might fall to the principal. There are endless headaches and problems associated to deliver a good program. Most coaches are not full-time employees, which is very problematic for a school.

Chapter 6: Technology: Its Joys and Woes!—Technology has introduced amazing innovations into schools, but it is fraught with problems and hazards. Many school handbooks have more pages dedicated to the responsible use of technology than any other topic. Counselors have identified more socially awkward children who are addicted to technology. Even Pope Francis has commented on the obsession that people have with their phones and other devices. While technology is here to stay, young people are constantly discovering new and dangerous avenues to traverse from a moral life of faith. Administrators are ever vigilant for abuses and hurtful activities that students pursue.

Chapter 7: Who Is Going to Pay What It Costs?—As the coronavirus leaves a financial disaster in its wake, many wonder who is going to have the money to sustain these schools? Even in the best of times, parents rarely pay the full cost to educate a child. Pastors are increasingly apprehensive to fund schools especially when the school families do not go to darken the doors of the church on Sunday. Financial stability is probably the common denominator for a school's success or failure.

Chapter 8: Liturgy and Service Projects—A goal of Catholic education should be encouraging active and lifelong participation in one's parish community. Young people enjoy performing service projects and unfortunately this has sometimes become the chief identifier of evidence of Catholicism. Certainly, charitable acts are core to the faith, but have they eclipsed prayer and the Mass?

Luke Rosiak has completed a book entitled *Race to the Bottom: Uncovering the Secret Forces Destroying American Public Education* (2022). His grim assessment of government education and how it has chronically failed the poor for decades makes a strong case for School Choice. In it, he cites research that affirms many parents across the nation want excellent schools and School Choice just like the privileged and politicians provide for their children. Meaningful School Choice could be a game changer for Catholic schools, but it will not solve all the problems.

Catholic schools are facing mighty headwinds from the finances and the adversarial culture wars that plague American society and often tear at Gospel values and Church teachings. Clear thinking and faith-filled leadership is needed more than ever to strengthen the schools so that they may be responsible beneficiaries of this amazing legacy that spans the American story. There is no question that the schools, or some of the schools will survive, but the vitality and determination of previous generations seems to have waned. Those schools built before the 1970s were the result of hard work and sacrifice with a vision that the schools would survive and thrive.

As the Church stumbled through Vatican II and its repercussions, coupled with the unrest of the 1960s, parish involvement began to wane, and Catholics moved out of urban neighborhoods into the suburbs where Catholic schools were few and families were content to send their children to the government schools. Consideration of these external challenges set the table to better examine the internal challenges that school leaders are facing today and whether Catholics today have the energy, fortitude, and conviction to stabilize the schools and provide for their growth.

Chapter 1

How We Got to This Point with Catholic Schools

Background

This chapter's presentation has three objectives. First, to provide a turbo-speed tour of the story of Catholic schools in the United States with some surprising facts as well as some information that might be common knowledge, along with some of the leaders who shaped the future. Second, to present some current data on the schools. Third, to identify the very serious questions facing our schools, our Church leaders (current and future), and the People of God, and that will be discussed in the subsequent chapters. Undoubtedly, each reader has personal views and perspectives on Catholic schools as shaped by your experience and/or perspective. What is being presented here are the general trends across the United States, and where we find most of our schools, i.e., in the urban areas. No doubt you the reader will develop questions and prognostications as you saunter through this material.

The story of Catholic schools begins with the bigger story of Catholic education in America and the effort to convert a continent to Christianity which began over five centuries ago with the arrival of Christopher Columbus. Anyone who remembers their American History courses will recall that this period is usually given scant treatment in textbooks. This period is often dominated by the English colonies and events leading up to and preparing for the American Revolution. Kevin Starr's *Continental Ambitions: Roman Catholics in North America: The Colonial Experience* (2016) details the Catholic experience through the Spanish, French, and English recusants. This carefully researched study awakens one from the amnesia of these vastly different approaches to evangelization and catechesis from coast to coast and from north to south.

Most of these were evangelization efforts, like the North American Martyrs in Upper New York and Canada, were attempts to evangelize the indigenous people. (These were the original North American Martyrs, not to be confused with the soccer team mascots at the Pontifical North American College in Rome.) Among the better-known leaders of this era might be the missionaries to New France who were brutally martyred by those they were seeking to evangelize. The names of St. Isaac Jogues, the first priest in what is now New York State, and Saint Jean de Brebeuf are among the most recognized leaders of this missionary project. Jesuits from Spain and Italy also established missions in Florida and reaching to Baja California. It is interesting to note that many of these missions in Mexico bear the names of Jesuit saints and important devotions: San Luis Gonzaga, San Javier, San Ignacio, and Loreto.

The distinctive Catholic legacy of Alta California is irreversibly manifested in its cities' names like Santa Monica, San Fernando, San Gabriel, Santa Barbara, and San Francisco. These all began as mission stations founded by eighteenth-century Franciscans under the leadership of Saint Junipero Serra who began his ministry in 1768. These missions were a continuation of the project begun earlier by the Jesuits; however, the Jesuits and Franciscans had very different strategies for evangelization. The colonial missions were centers for catechetical, vocational, and agricultural education, as well as foundations for imparting liturgical and musical training.

Though the missions, their purpose, and their administration have come under intense scholarly debate in recent years, even to the point of questioning what was once thought to be the saintly character of Serra himself, these missions provided the symbolic establishment of the Catholic faith with the catechetical and educational charter at the very founding of the various cities. The educational thrust of these missions was aimed primarily at Native Americans and those California Catholics who were native Mexicans, as well as the small Spanish immigrant population.

Many may wonder why the Jesuits did not continue establishing the missions northward into Alta California. Pope Clement XIV suppressed the Society of Jesus in 1773. Jesuits throughout the world had to renounce their vows and became diocesan priests, like Archbishop John Carroll; some were driven into exile, and some left the priesthood altogether. The suppression lasted until 1814, when a beleaguered Pope Pius VII restored the Society. Clement XIV had caved into the wills of several crowned heads of Europe and others within the Church who harbored hatred and unfavorable views of the Society. Clement and others mistakenly thought that the Jesuits had accumulated and were sheltering untold wealth in the New World, and when money speaks, few are deaf especially in Rome. Hence, the northern expansion of the missions was chiefly entrusted to the Franciscans and Dominicans.

In 1727 the Ursuline nuns arrived in New Orleans to educate young women in the struggling settlement. The school shunned the social and racial boundaries of early colonial society. Serving communities of slave and free, black and white, the school generated the highest literacy rates among the European colonies of the New World. "This school which was founded by the Sisters of the Order of Saint Ursula, the Ursuline Academy of New Orleans enjoys the distinction of being both the oldest, continuously-operating school for girls and the oldest Catholic school in the United States."[1]

Archbishop John Carroll (1735–1815), the first US bishop, had an expansive vision for Catholic schools in the United States. He established Georgetown University in 1789. The Catholic population had to get used to being one religion among many, with no special privileges or protections. Carroll had a vision to assimilate, and the architectural choice of his Assumption cathedral demonstrates this. The design of the cathedral is Neoclassical, which was the current style of choice throughout the new republic. Carroll enlisted the help of Elizabeth Ann Seton (1774–1821) who would later be the first native-born citizen of the United States to be canonized. While we ascribe to her the title of patroness of Catholic schools in the United States, she did not start them. However, her growing community of sisters advanced the mission in a mighty way.[2]

There are many giants in this story of the development of Catholic schools. In 1829 Mother Mary Elizabeth Lange (1789–1882) along with Father James Nicholas Joubert, SS, founded the Oblate Sisters of Providence whose purpose was to care for and educate African American children. In the south Henriette DeLille (1813–1862) founded the Catholic order of the Sisters of the Holy Family in New Orleans, which was composed of free women of color. The order provided nursing care and a home for orphans, later establishing schools as well. In 1989 the order formally opened its cause with the Vatican in the canonization of Henriette DeLille. She was declared venerable in 2010.

The tsunami of Irish immigrants landed in the nineteenth century when over eight million people came to the United States (Moran, G. P. 2004). Jay Dolan described the Irish portion of this immigration figure:

> Long before the potato blight, people had been leaving Ireland in rather impressive numbers; in fact, between 1820 and 1840, more than 260,000 Irish emigrated to America. Once the famine struck, however, the exodus escalated dramatically, and in a brief, six-year, period, 1846–51, over 1 million people left Ireland. The passing of the famine hardly halted the flow of migration, with the result that, between 1851 and 1920, 3.3 million Irish immigrants settled in the United States, bringing the total Irish migration to the United States, during this hundred-year period, 1820–1920, to 4.3 million people. (p. 128)

Diane Ravitch (1988) lucidly illustrated the paradigm that is replicated through the history of the nation by looking at New York City in the 1790s:

> Though the town of New York had not yet experienced any large-scale immigration, native New Yorkers already associated immigration with crime and poverty. There was a reality to their attitude, since newcomers were more likely to be poor than the native-born, and most criminals were reported to be foreigners. There is no more constant theme in the unfolding of New York City's history than the reciprocal relationship between the native and the immigrant: the immigrant arrives poor, lives in crowded slums with others like himself, suffers discrimination and terrible living conditions, and (as a group) produces a disproportionate number of criminals and paupers; the native blames the immigrant for bringing crime, poverty, and slums to the city, discriminates against him, and wonders whether *this* particular group can ever be assimilated into American society. With each major wave of immigration—Irish, Italians, Jews, blacks, Puerto-Ricans—the scenario has been replayed. And in each instance, the cultural clash of the old and the new has occurred in and around the school. (p. 5–6)

It was considered that being Catholic was irreconcilable with being a good US citizen. In Philadelphia, the Bible Riots of the 1840s arose from the compulsory reading of the King James Version of the scriptures in public schools, a version that was repugnant to immigrant Catholics who fled persecution at the hands of oppressive British policies. When Archbishop Francis Kenrick (1796–1863) appealed to the competent authorities to use the Catholic-approved Douai-Rheims version for the Roman Catholic students and those students be excused from Protestant catechetical classes, tensions ignited. Churches were burned and the militia was called to restore order. The common schools of this period were undisputedly Protestant schools and financed with public funds (Ravitch, D. 1988). Textbooks and lessons were full of contemptuous illustrations and examples that derided Catholicism and subjected its young adherents to lessons that undermined the faith of their families.

Archbishop John Hughes (1797–1864) was known as *Dagger John*. (This inflammatory nickname is more popularly associated with his fiery temper and passion for his flock; however, the reality is not quite as exciting as the myth; when a bishop signs his name on a document, it is preceded by the symbol of the Holy Cross. Hence, Archbishop Hughes's signature cross resembled a dagger, and given his pugnacious temperament that may have been intentional.)

Hughes, like Kenrick in Philadelphia, was an immigrant from Ireland and fought these same battles in New York but with a different strategy. Unlike Archbishop Carroll who wanted American Catholics to fit in, Hughes wanted to check the rising antipathy towards the Irish Catholics by emphasizing the rights of his Catholic flock among the dominant Protestant citizens. This was demonstrated in architectural contrast to the Neo-classical Cathedral of the Assumption in Baltimore.

When Hughes designed the new St. Patrick's on a countryside meadow of what is now Midtown Manhattan, he chose a massive neo-Gothic design, a style that is essentially Roman Catholic. When rumors reached Hughes that Catholic properties were at risk of arson, as in Philadelphia, he warned the nativist mayor: "*Should one Catholic come to harm, or should one Catholic Church or business be molested, we shall turn his city into a second Moscow*" (Ravitch, 1988, p. 36). Hughes's allusion to Moscow was the generally known fact that the citizens of Moscow preferred self-destruction, rather than allow Napoleon access and use of the city; this reference was not lost on the New York establishment who knew Hughes to be man of his word and a force to be reckoned with. Civil unrest was avoided, and Hughes would turn his attention to establishing Catholic schools and education as a means of advancing the plight of the poor.

Parish schools were being established in several large cities such as Philadelphia, Baltimore, and New York. Hughes made a case for distributing those taxes which were collected for education according to the school chosen by the family, so the money would follow the child and benefit the school. Hughes entered public debates to plead this cause, but the measure ultimately failed. Yet, efforts began to neutralize the seditious and impertinent Catholic references found in the schools and particularly in textbooks. These strategies to neutralize the religious differences eventually would lead to slowly secularizing these essentially Protestant schools and that process of secularization remains an area of debate to this day.

Anti-Catholicism was a growing sentiment among the Nativists. This stance even applied to employment; the phrase *No Irish Need Apply* was widely and proudly utilized. Samuel F. B. Morse, best known for his invention of the telegraph, held Catholics in disdain and sought ways to minimize opportunities for Catholics. Morse promoted these sentiments in popular leaflets of the day. Further, these anti-Catholic attitudes, which were synonymous with anti-immigration or nativist agendas, were institutionalized within the ranks of the Know-Nothing Party, which grew in the 1850s. These anti-Catholic attitudes were often mirrored in the policies and platforms of the Republican Party.

President Ulysses S. Grant made the following remark in Des Moines, Iowa (1876), which would further fuel a bias against funding of religious schools and of course was a clear signal to his audience of not assisting Catholic schools:

> Encourage free schools and resolve that not one dollar of the money appropriated to their support shall be appropriated to the support of any sectarian school; that neither the state or nation, not both combined, shall support institutions of learning other than those sufficient to afford to every child in the land

the opportunity of a good common-school education, unmixed with sectarian, pagan, or atheistical dogma. (Strauss, V. 2019)

Republican Representative James G. Blaine from Maine would propose an amendment (1875) to the United States Constitution banning any public funding for religious schools, but it failed passage. Nonetheless, the enthusiasm for this "Blaine Amendment" would spread to 38 states and find a way into the state constitutions, since education is specifically a financial responsibility of the state. The 10th Amendment of the United States Constitution gives to the states the responsibility of education, since it is not covered in the Constitution ("The powers not delegated to the United States by the Constitution, nor prohibited by it to the States, are reserved to the States respectively, or to the people"). The Blaine amendments are seemingly insurmountable and are imbued with a nascent anti-Catholic purpose.

Though not always mentioned, Catholic schools were the target for the proposals of Grant and Blaine. Both Grant and Blaine were among a growing number of Americans who were vocal about their anti-Catholic positions. Furthermore, the congressional record on the Blaine Amendment debates reveals (1) the underlying anti-Catholic sentiment among amendment advocates and (2) the focus of the amendment on Catholic schools. (Hart, Y. 2004)

Almost a decade later (1884) James G. Blaine would build upon this Catholic prejudice as he championed the Republican aversion to Rum (embracing the temperance movement), Romanism (the xenophobic Geist aimed at Catholic immigrants), and Rebellion (a reference to the Civil War and playing on people's fears) in his failed campaign for the presidency against the Democratic nominee and winner, Grover Cleveland. Blaine wanted to exploit the anti-Catholic feelings of the time but was roundly defeated even as Catholic immigrants would continue to flood into the country. However, even though these Catholic immigrant groups may have shared a common religion, those with a bit of seniority in the new country did not welcome the newcomers wholeheartedly.

It is good to remember in all discussions around funding of education and its administration that education is a *National Interest*, a *State's Responsibility*, and a *Local Duty*. These distinctions are useful to see where roadblocks exist to School Choice initiatives, especially with the Blaine amendments firmly rooted in the constitutions of most states. Seeing the futility of accessing public funding for parochial schools, bishops developed an alternate strategy to educate its children.

The bishops of the United States, concerned about the diminution of the faith and the importance of getting an education to move forward in society, addressed the importance of parochial schools at the Third Plenary Council of Baltimore in 1884. Among their mandates was the establishment of a Catholic school in every parish where it was feasible. Orders of sisters, brothers, and priests were burgeoning with new recruits and most of their energies would focus upon Catholic schools. The religious men and women would respond to this mandate and build the second-largest educational enterprise in the United States. However, as the years would pass and Catholics took their place in the comfortable middle class, all the hard-won lessons of the immigrant forebears became foggy, unimportant, and not shared.

As immigrant people are socialized into a new culture, a typical pattern of identification with the dominant culture transpires. The first thing to go is the language of the former country. *"You have to learn English if you want to get anywhere,"* was a common reprimand to the children of immigrants. So, often enough, immigrants would not teach their children or grandchildren their native tongue. Next, religion would be gradually abandoned. Not surprisingly, the last thing to be abandoned, if it would be abandoned at all, is food. Recipes and flavors would somehow be in the DNA and carried forward. This did not bode well for Catholic schools when religion and the parish would no longer be the center of the neighborhood and family's activities.

Sister Dolores Liptak, RSM, illustrated the importance of national parishes and their impact on the various immigrant groups from Europe in the late nineteenth and early twentieth centuries.[3] She asserted that these parishes added greatly to the self-confidence of a people that might have lost not only the faith, but their personal pride regarding their ethnic background. Language and culture went hand in hand and German immigrants were especially attentive to this reality in the dominant Irish American Catholic culture. The French Canadians, Poles, and Lithuanians were eager to establish these parish schools; the Italians were a bit late to the project and valued their children entering the workforce.

These groups also brought along clergy and religious who could relate to their fellow immigrants. These priests and sisters were highly regarded because they were typically the most educated people in the community, but they would help preserve language and customs. Saint Francis Xavier Cabrini initially wanted to serve as a missionary to China, but Pope Leo XIII directed his energies to serve the Italian immigrants in the United States. Many religious orders of sisters, brothers, and priests have histories laboring with fellow immigrants.

One group that made a connection to the past, or had not forgotten the Gospel values of serving the poor and welcoming the stranger in heroic ways, were the religious sisters. The sisters provided an eager and ready workforce to staff the growing number of schools, especially in urban areas. In the first half of the twentieth century active religious communities of women were attracting large numbers of vocations.

The young women who entered religious life would be prepared to serve primarily either in health care or education. 1965 was a peak year with over 111,000 sisters serving in parochial schools; they comprised the backbone workforce of the educational mission. However, this army of workers would almost suddenly disappear, leaving the schools in financial straits signaling not only the decline of their orders but also the diminishment of schools. What happened?

The confluence of many powerful forces threw the Church into a state of confusion under the aegis of renewal. The Second Vatican Council asked all religious communities to adopt a program of reflection and renewal to adapt to needs of the modern world. This renewal led many orders down a path of dissolution towards extinction. Many new ministries opened to sisters and teaching in schools was not seen as a cutting-edge assignment. Also, many communities allowed sisters to find and select their own ministries. Hence, sisters left the schools in droves. At the same time the pipeline of new vocations was drying up. As fewer recruits were entering religious life, many women were exiting religious life altogether, outpacing the numbers entering, and a stage was set for communities composed of elderly women.

While the sisters drew a very small salary for teaching, the system was built in such a way as to operate schools on their generous service. As schools had to hire more teachers with escalating salaries and benefits, it became increasingly impossible for many parishes to operate an elementary school. Consolidations and closures followed, and the period of growth and expansion transitioned rapidly into a long hospice-like trajectory of decline for many schools. The Catholic schools of the United States were built with the presumption of low operating costs and the contributed services of religious women and men. As the teaching sisters, brothers, and priests said farewell to this ministry, the schools they staffed often enough followed with closure within a few years, but obviously not all did as capable lay women and men stepped forward to carry the mission forward.

As the Church in the United States crossed the threshold of the new millennium, the diminishment of Catholic schools continues to this day. As the calendar reached the new millennium in 2000, the devastating clergy sex abuse crisis was about to sweep across the United States beginning in Boston and drawing every diocese into the reckoning. Pope Saint John Paul II was able to lead the Church into this new era as he had desired and prayed despite his growing frailty following a vigorous reign. Pope Benedict XVI would succeed him in 2005 and continue to teach and promote an authentic interpretation of Vatican II amidst growing disaffection for organized religion and special contempt for Catholicism. A new paradigm for reporting on the Catholic Church came into vogue; newspapers and the media would lead with lurid stories of the priesthood and criticism of the Church's governance. At a time of expanding social media platforms and instant access to the news, more and more Catholics were opting out of active participation in parishes. Young people were being formed more by the dominant values presented by social media, music, and the entertainment world.

On February 11, 2013, the world was startled by the resignation announcement of Pope Benedict XVI, a move that no living person could have imagined. In the conclave that followed, Jorge Cardinal Bergoglio, a Jesuit from Argentina, was elected to guide the Church, taking the name of Francis after the much-loved saint of Assisi. Pope Francis had a common touch that resonated with the world.

Some of his impromptu press conferences on various flights often opened cans of worms regarding faith and morals as unsophisticated reporters sought a headline-grabbing sound bite and would quote him out of context. Many of those settled questions in the Church now seemed open for discussion as the Church prepares for a Synod in Rome with diocesan synods to take place prior to the big one in 2023; and the secular press was salivating over the opportunity to shape the image of Francis using some of these random comments.

Covid-19 has played havoc across the globe and made unusual demands on church attendance. Going back to the Ten Commandments, keeping holy the Sabbath has been interpreted by Catholics as an obligation to attend Sunday Mass. As parishes restricted Mass attendance and/or encouraged people to participate via live stream, many church-going folks grew comfortable with this arrangement, enjoying a Bloody Mary while watching Mass on TV and switching channels to check sporting events. However, when people were invited back to the pews, many have not responded. One pastor recalled running into a missing parishioner at a liquor store who was embarrassed to be seen by her shepherd. She was tongue-tied trying to explain her absence at Mass. He assured her that the church was sanitized thoroughly before each Mass and was certainly cleaner than this liquor store. In short, Mass attendance has plummeted even further, and it is hard to imagine that it will come back soon.

It is not just the disappearance of those practicing their faith, but the outright rejection of the faith. A not so unusual example was at a Catholic high school assembly presenting a pro-life message and the majority of students walked out in protest over a settled question in Church morality.[4] In November 2021, a student organization at Loyola Marymount University in Los Angeles hosted a fundraiser for Planned Parenthood; one must wonder how this got past the leadership of the school and who is minding the mission? These are but two examples of the growing disconnect between the Catholic mission of Catholic schools and those who use them.

The *Wall Street Journal* cited a study that claimed: "*Half of people between 13 and 25 surveyed by a nonprofit said they felt out of sync with their houses of worship on race, gender, immigration and more*."⁵ Of course one would have to wonder how well catechized are these young, disaffected people? Even Catholics who attended Catholic school may be poorly informed about what they are turning their noses up at. If Tik-Tok, Facebook, and Twitter supply nonstop information from an iPhone, and the dominant values of the entertainment industry are the principal sources of nonstop formation, how could the Bible, the Catechism of the Catholic Church, or an encyclical make much difference? Hence, these are just a few of the challenges facing the Church and Catholic school leaders in the United States today regarding the formation and education of young people.

In 1964 a book was published that wadled into the booming Catholic school world like an overactive skunk spraying its way on every wall: *Are Parochial Schools the Answer? Catholic Education in Light of the Council,* by Mary Perkins Ryan. Ryan was a journalist and mother of five children who attended Catholic and government schools. Her conclusion and response to the question proposed by the book's title was a resounding "NO." This book was a combination of prophecy, practicality, and a naive euphoria that was so ubiquitous among the enthusiasts of Vatican II and especially the American branch of the *soixante-huitard* who embraced many zany experiments with the liturgy.

Perkins Ryan herself had been an active participant in many liturgical movements and was delighted that the first document to emerge from the Ecumenical Council was *Sacrosanctum Concilium,* the Constitution on the Liturgy. As a constitution, it carried the greatest weight of the teaching authority of the world's bishops in union with the pope as compared to some of the other documents. Though most people had no idea how the reformed liturgy would be structured, she was jubilant at thinking about the possibilities, and the Mass would be the centerpiece of her catechetical reform and exodus, gradual as it might be, from Catholic schools.

She was keenly aware of the construction campaigns from coast to coast and the expense of building and renovating schools. She felt the amount of money, time, and energy poured into Catholic schools was a misappropriation of funds for so few. She rightly noted that it would be impossible for every Catholic child to be in a Catholic school. To her, the time of priests, brothers, sisters, and yes, even bishops would be better spent on religious education programs for children and at Newman Centers at public universities in addition to other emerging ministries. She described the genesis and growth of Catholic schools as the result of a "siege mentality" that guided their establishment through the nineteenth century and into the twentieth.

Now that Catholics "had arrived" in society and were entering the middle class, the siege should be declared over. The continuation of Catholic schools is a misplaced emphasis that is really a relic of the past. Catholic children should be in public schools thereby sharing the diversity of the population and building upon the ecumenical themes that unite people and avoid focusing on the issues that divide congregations. There can be no doubt that the 1961 election of John F. Kennedy as the first Catholic president represented a point of arrival and acceptance of Catholics.

What was particularly daring in this book was that it was written as the Catholic school system was nearing its zenith. Convent novitiates that supplied the vast majority of teachers for the elementary schools and many high schools were bursting at the seams. The same was true for the novitiates of orders of religious men, both clerical and the brothers. Seminaries were overflowing with vocations. Many religious orders began expanding their motherhouses and formation facilities to accommodate the long line of applicants. If there was a siege mentality in the church and in its schools, new recruits were excited to step into action and answer the call. Perkins Ryan could not predict the precipice of cataclysmic deterioration that the universal church was approaching.

Men and women were attending Mass in record numbers in the early 1960s. From the perspective of many people, the church was strong and certain. The Catholic school network developed because of the vision, hard work, and generosity of generations of believers. Perkins Ryan was advocating more of a revolution to repurpose Catholic schools and redeploy the vast workforce of nuns, priests, and brothers to other ministries, but not exclusive of catechetical work. She wisely anticipated that there would be resistance to her line of thinking and that there would always be some Catholic schools; however, she did not anticipate the diminishment of the schools in quite the evolutionary process that unfolded. This trajectory of decline does not seem to have a leveling off or endpoint of stabilization.

Again, Mary Perkins Ryan believed that there would always be Catholic schools, though she begrudgingly expressed that prediction as concession to the entrenched devotees. Siege or no siege, many Catholics in the United States have been convinced that the parochial schools are the best means to transmit the faith. It would be hard to find leaders in the Church who would be crowing about the state of religious education programs, both in the Catholic schools and in the weekend CCD (Confraternity of Christian Doctrine) classes, but at least the schools offer more time and a vibrant culture to promote the faith. One can consider the dismay of the United States Conference of Catholic Bishops over the teaching of the Eucharist at their 2021 meetings.

Various polling agencies have uncovered wide swaths of either total ignorance about the sacrament of Holy Eucharist or a complete rejection of the official teachings regarding it. This barren fig tree cannot be a surprise to many when one considers the continual march out of the Church. The recliner and *New York Times* or Sunday brunch and/or football is a preferable liturgical exercise than the pew and attention to the altar. So, what kind of catechesis is that? When the sacrament of Confirmation is celebrated, there is a clear understanding that with this adult step, one is to continue their study and deepen their knowledge of scripture and the teachings of the Church. How can such profound beliefs be covered in a ten-minute homily or sermon once a week? But at least by regularly attending Mass, Catholics place themselves in the proximity of hearing the faith proclaimed. Saint Paul wrote in Romans (10:14): "How then are they to call on Him in whom they have not believed? How are they to believe in Him whom they have not heard? And how are they to hear without a preacher?"

Perkins Ryan also took aim at the catechetics of the time which would have been the Baltimore Catechism; this was a book of straightforward questions and straightforward answers. No, it did not afford much room for discussion or speculation, but it did provide a solid basis of belief that could be pondered and better appreciated with maturation and inquiry. Felt banners, banal guitar music and sentimental hymns telling God how great "we" are, and puppet and clown Masses certainly did not fill a void but contributed to the collapse of the worshipping community.

Recognizing the disorganized thinking, albeit well-intentioned, that followed Vatican II, Pope John Paul II decreed that a Catechism of the Catholic Church be written; it was issued in 1992. This book is a basic summary of all the beliefs of the Catholic Church and provides a center of catechetical gravity on which religion textbooks could be based. Twenty-plus years after its promulgation, the goal of a church composed of a well-informed body of believers is still rather illusive.

Many people have mistakenly thought that Rod Dreher's book, *The Benedict Option: A Strategy for Christians in a Post-Christian Nation* dealt with the teachings of Pope Benedict XVI; however, this was a reference to Saint Benedict, one of the Patron Saints of Europe and the founder of Western monasticism. St. Benedict fled the decaying sixth-century Roman Empire for the countryside to settle down with like-minded believers and live a life of poverty, chastity, and obedience. Dreher suggests that this may be the best route given the current times which are adversarial to organized religion. Interestingly, Pope Benedict XVI saw a diminished church as well.

Benedict commented:

> Let us go a step farther. From the crisis of today the Church of tomorrow will emerge—a Church that has lost much. She will become small and will have to start afresh more or less from the beginning. She will no longer be able to inhabit many of the edifices she built in prosperity. As the number of her

adherents diminishes, so it will lose many of her social privileges. In contrast to an earlier age, it will be seen much more as a voluntary society, entered only by free decision. As a small society, it will make much bigger demands on the initiative of her individual members. Undoubtedly it will discover new forms of ministry and will ordain to the priesthood approved Christians who pursue some profession. In many smaller congregations or in self-contained social groups, pastoral care will normally be provided in this fashion. Along-side this, the full-time ministry of the priesthood will be indispensable as formerly. But in all the changes at which one might guess, the Church will find her essence afresh and with full conviction in that which was always at her center: faith in the triune God, in Jesus Christ, the Son of God made man, in the presence of the Spirit until the end of the world. In faith and prayer, she will again recognize the sacraments as the worship of God and not as a subject for liturgical scholarship. (2021)

Perhaps this is the situation in which the Church finds itself vis-à-vis Catholic schools. Are the schools a hindrance to building up the faith community and a tremendous financial burden? Or might these schools be one of the last opportunities to cultivate a life of faith, hope, and love in the students. Certainly, the abandonment of the schools as Perkins Ryan envisioned would do much harm to the communities of faith and there is certainly no magic program waiting to be unveiled that is going to solve all the problems associated with a disappearing flock.

These problems sadly include a divided Catholic Church regarding beliefs and morals. As a growing number of people self-describe as spiritual but not religious, that disposition does not include being active in the community of believers. It saves one from contributing and supporting the parish projects which would include a school. More and more, people are quite comfortable creating their own system of beliefs. Divine Revelation has little to do with how one packages one's beliefs. This attitude is evident in many families who choose to send their children to Catholic schools and get upset with school leaders when certain truths conflict with what the parents hold as true. Unlike the battles of old where newly arrived Catholics were pitted against non-Catholics, some of the bigger battles are fought among the members. But there are other challenges.

Finding committed, practicing Catholics to fill leadership roles and teaching positions is a growing challenge. While there are committed practicing Catholics, many have chosen other career paths, and some of these include working in government schools where salaries are typically better along with the benefits that are paid. That is not to say that a Catholic school professional will be on the welfare rolls, but many will attest that their families cannot afford some of the private Catholic schools given their salary. And just as many families are not on the same page with the Church's teachings, so it is true for many who have been hired over the years as well as for current applicants. In the hiring process, applicants will often tell the employer whatever they think that person wants to hear; after the contract is signed, a different story may emerge.

The days of a reliable pipeline of religious sisters, brothers, and priests to staff the schools ended decades ago. Some schools still have a relationship with an order, but typically the number of religious from that community will be small. Provincials of some communities that have not raised the white flag of defeat with the project will attempt to cover a few leadership positions, but with dwindling vocations, meeting the need with such a thin bench is daunting if not impossible. As a remedy, some orders that sponsor schools try to direct the boards by requiring a certain number of members, but this can be a full-time ministry for a few members who are rapidly advancing in age and diminishing health.

The schools need to offer a full menu of co-curricular activities and athletics that takes the lion's share of after-school activities. There are considerable costs involved with running successful athletic programs, but these sports also have a great capacity to build school spirit and unify a community; so there are tremendous benefits, and chief among them would be the unique learning opportunities that they teach. Along with the many benefits are new challenges that can vex school leaders, especially with finding the right personnel who will be supportive of the school's mission; while this sounds like a simple no-brainer, it is not as easy to configure as one might think.

Technology has introduced amazing innovations into the schools but can also be viewed as Trojan Horses bearing endless migraines for school leaders and students. Digital textbooks that lighten a student's backpack load, the speedy exchange of feedback with teachers, and apps that support various courses like a dry lab to dissect a frog, are all amazing benefits. However, many problems have been brought along as well with bullying on social media and students being in a mode of perpetual distraction for wanting to check their phones, iPads, etc.

Finally, finances will be a perpetual challenge and may well be the undoing and closing of many schools in the future if the current trajectory is an accurate forecast; no school has closed because of a robust enrollment and merrily operating in the black. Financial challenges have always been the wolf at the door of the Catholic school project. Operational costs will only increase and cause many to reach for the smelling salts as they consider the escalations. School leaders who must send the dreaded letter each spring announcing the percentage increase of tuition do so with clenched teeth awaiting blowback from many of the families, which is not in rare supply.

These are just some of the perennial challenges facing Catholic schools that will be explored in subsequent chapters. No doubt, these and many other challenges await the leaders of Catholic schools in the future. The history demonstrates several recurring themes of determination driven by strong faith convictions. When these are in place, generosity and sacrifice are not far behind, but walking alongside these will be indifference and a lack of appreciation for what has been built. How the church will respond to these challenges is a story that is being written now.

NOTES

1. Ursuline Academy n.d.
2. Recently two very fine books were published about Saint Elizabeth Ann Seton. Kathleen Sprows Cummings (2019): *A Saint of Our Own: How the Quest for a Holy Hero Helped Catholics Become American*; and Catherine O'Donnell (2018): *Elizabeth Seton: American Saint.*
3. Liptak 1989
4. Olivera 2021
5. Ansberry 2021

Chapter 2

"I Thought that This Was Supposed to Be a Catholic School?" (Parents and Mission)

The quote chosen for the title of this chapter represents an accusation that every Catholic school administrator has heard when a student gets into serious trouble and especially if that student is asked to leave the school. Despite the popular perception that students are asked to leave Catholic schools for frivolous infractions such as chewing gum, saying a naughty word, or being late for school, the reality is quite different.

Students in Catholic schools face all the problems and difficulties that are part of growing up in the new millennium: easy access to alcohol and drugs, bullying, racism, improper use of social media, breakdown of the family, psychological problems, suicide ideation, and a growing secularization, to name but a few. When students get crossways with a school's code of conduct, the school usually goes to extremes to make the situation a learning and formational experience and the school strives to keep the student enrolled. It is a rare and painful experience to ask a student to leave the school and is only done in the most egregious cases.

In high schools under the principal/president model of governance, the principal handles such disciplinary cases that rise to a possibility of expulsion; in elementary schools, it is always the principal, along with the pastor's support. When the principal and deans decide it is in the best interest of the community that a student be expelled, that is done with the backing and blessing of the president (the CEO of the school). Some schools have a rule that if some "new" evidence of innocence is brought forward, that was not considered in the case's adjudication, the family can ask the president to overturn the case.

Therefore, a disciplinary case is always vetted by the leadership of the school to make sure that all the leaders of the school are on the same page before the outcome is announced. It is at this point that the school leaders are lectured about the tenets of the Catholic faith by the culprit and family: "What would Jesus do? What happened to forgiveness? Wouldn't Pope Francis be appalled at the decision?, etc." The appeals are always formulaic and will ultimately plead and ask about ". . . this being a Catholic school." Or one might be questioned on it being a Jesuit school or Marist school, as though they operate as a parallel Church.

Consider this hypothetical case. A young high school student, "Myrna," learned the art of baking while developing excellent entrepreneurial skills. She baked brownies laced with marijuana. Myrna set up a small network of salesclerks in various schools to distribute the treats to help adolescents face and endure the rigors and tedium of the school day. When her business was discovered, she was asked to leave her school, and the parents were advised to get counseling for her. The parents were incensed by the callous dismissal and pleaded for forgiveness. Forgiveness was granted by the school, along with a hope that the girl would mend her ways and get a fresh start elsewhere.

She had transgressed many school rules and her dealings with the drug supplier placed many in harm's way; who knows where her dealer is in a drug organization and the dangerous people hiding in the shadows? School administrators are particularly sensitive to infractions that place the school community and others in danger, not to mention tarnishing the reputation of the school. Dealing with drugs always places a person in a web of illegal activities and shady people. Cities and states are rushing to legalize marijuana and monetize the sales; does this sound like bread and circuses from ancient Rome to anyone? Has not this same government been waging war on smoking of any kind because of its carcinogenic effects?

This gateway drug is especially dangerous for adolescents whose brains and physical development are several years from completion. Yet, the same parents pleading for their student's continued education at a Catholic school do not care so much about the hard facts of the school's rules and what science has to say about such a topic.

From their start, Catholic schools have had a dual mission here in America: to serve the community through an excellent education and to pass on the faith. Both were essential. It is a curious reality about why parents choose a Catholic school. Usually, the top reason is either the superior academics, the moral standards that are professed, or the safety that the school provides.

Sadly, and too often, the Catholicity of the school falls somewhere much lower in the ranking of why a family chooses a Catholic school, so one of those historic missions is still valued. This should not be a surprise with the growing trend of fewer people regularly attending Sunday Mass.

Ask any Catholic school teacher what their impressions are regarding the attendance of their students at Sunday Mass. Some faculty members attempt a discussion on Monday about the scripture readings and insights from the homilies from the weekend.

In the not too distant past many students might have been embarrassed at the prospect of being discovered for choosing to sleep over going to Sunday Mass, however, currently it is as neutral as saying you prefer tea rather than coffee with breakfast. COVID and being excused from the Sunday obligation have done irreparable harm to church attendance, and weekly attendance was not increasing before the pandemic.

Sunday Mass attendance will likely take a major hit when the pandemic finally subsides. The obligation to attend Sunday Mass is not of human origin; keeping holy the Sabbath came directly from God to Moses. In the Christian dispensation, Sunday became the day of the Sabbath, and Catholics have held the best way to honor this commandment is by participation in the Sacrifice of the Mass. Even at the institution of the Sacrament of the Eucharist, Jesus commands: "Do this in memory of me."

The faithful will have grown very comfortable watching Mass from the comfort of their living rooms and who does not enjoy a quiet, thorn-free Sunday morning? One can hope and pray for a spiritual awakening, but the ascendency of the secular agenda and its embrace by the political world, the eager promotion of the media and entertainment industry, does not augur well for such an awakening.

The Benedict Option[1] cited in chapter 1 and proposed by Rod Dreher foresees a much smaller Christian community and one that will be on the receiving end of powerful adversaries. And while school parents may not always be engaged in the faith life of the parish, they participate and take leadership roles in the school. So, in some places, the school can be the nexus for evangelization.

Years ago, sociologist James Coleman researched and described Social Capital as the important community relationships which help to form children. Coleman's book was a shot in the arm for beleaguered Catholic schools as it identified what everyone knew and probably took for granted but did not realize how it was a major descriptor of Catholic schools and something that would not be found as pervasively in government schools.

Parents continue to roll up their sleeves when a job needs to be done. The schools increasingly rely upon fundraising to close the gap between actual costs of running the school and the annual shortfall of what families are being charged, and this fundraising is typically accomplished by the leadership of parents. The dark side of this generous energy is that it is not unheard of to engender a sense of familiarity that leads to a misplaced sense of entitlement.

Some parents working closely with the school's leadership will often be in the building and develop a powerful set of working relationships with faculty and staff. Unfortunately, this sometimes leads some to thinking they know far better how to run the school, especially if some neuralgic point develops. Some observe that since everyone has spent many years in school, everyone is an expert on how to run a school.

More families than not sacrifice to send their children to Catholic schools. They are typically the supporters of three school systems: paying property taxes to fund the government schools which they have chosen not to use; contributing to parish and diocesan programs whose support helps the parish bottom line, and many schools beyond their parish throughout the diocese; and then there is the direct tuition paid to the school where they have children. It is a natural reaction to see how parents feel invested and want to offer advice on how things should be done.

Athletics are especially prone to parental entanglement. Most elementary school coaches are volunteers and do not enjoy the benefit of a stipend or salary that a high school coach would earn to help assuage the assault of a pushy parent. Why might parents of athletes be pushy? There are many possible reasons.

The coach does not see the amazing ability of their child and the coach is not using them sufficiently. Many parents have had success playing sports in their own school days and feel they know more about the sport than the coach, and they are not reticent to share how the team could improve.

Social media makes this even more problematic, with easy access to griping and sowing seeds of dissension and organizing petitions. Parents are also the biggest cheerleaders and supporters of these important activities and are typically delighted to host dinners, gatherings, and other events to build up the community. More on athletics in chapter 5.

As schools entered the seemingly endless Covid adaptations, many schools were being hectored by parents ". . . to close school! To get ahead of the plague! Be courageous! I thought we (i.e., this school) were supposed to be leaders!" When schools transitioned the school year into online learning, a different section of the chorus started a counter descant: "You're caving in to the media hysteria. We aren't paying for online learning! Will there be refunds or tuition reductions?" Working with parents is challenging! Sometimes you cannot win, and you cannot even tie!

A central truth and belief of Catholicism is that parents are the primary educators of their children. This is especially specified in the Baptismal liturgy. At the Blessing of the Father, the celebrant states: "God is the giver of all life, human and divine. May he bless the father of this child. He and his wife will be the first teachers of their child in the ways of faith. May they be also the best of teachers, bearing witness to the faith by what they say and do, in Christ Jesus our Lord."

Earlier in the liturgy, the parents are handed a candle which was lit from the Paschal candle. The celebrant offers this prayer to accompany the candle:

"Parents and godparents, this light is entrusted to you to be kept burning brightly. This child of yours has been enlightened by Christ. He (she) is to walk always as a child of the light. May he (she) keep the flame of faith alive in his (her) heart. When the Lord comes, may he (she) go out to meet him with all the saints in the heavenly kingdom."

It is hard to imagine a clearer understanding of the duties and goals of Catholic parents. Just about every official Church document dealing with education and catechesis will cite the fact that parents are the primary educators of their children. Hence, Catholic schools are resources to help the parents in their duties—the schools are not a substitute.

Perhaps one of the biggest challenges facing Catholic schools is why they should even exist in this day and age and the assumptions that guide their existence. A bishop once commented that the only time Catholics stand together is for the reading of the Gospel at Mass. Some of those assumptions would include: acceptance of Church teaching on faith and morals; active participation in the parish's life by attending weekly Mass and frequent reception of the Sacrament of Reconciliation; and these would be minimal signs to encourage the establishment of a parish school and to support it.

Ask any pastor about the attendance of school families at Sunday Mass; many are infrequent guests if they darken the doors at all. Given the colossal investment of resources it takes to run a school, many a pastor is flummoxed about the wisdom of the investment. Hence, some observe that many Catholic schools are becoming private schools with a religious mission that many families can tolerate, even though many beliefs are more reflective of a political party than those of the Church.

When one thinks of all the divisive issues swirling in the Church today which are adversarial to the assumptions mentioned, it is easy to spot irreconcilable differences. While Catholic leaders loathe the "S" word, (Schism), it seems that Catholics increasingly share very little with official teachings and are formed more by liberal news agencies, suggesting that a schism exists and there is scant hope for reconciliation.

One must wonder if the larger schism is destined for formalization. In recent memory it would not be a first when one considers the Old Catholic Church, the National Polish Catholic Church, and the unusual development of St. Stanislaus Parish in St. Louis, Missouri.

St. Stanislaus was established as a National Parish for the Polish and governed by a board of trustees. Archbishop Raymond Burke attempted to regularize the governance of the parish under the direction of the pastor and archdiocese, but this was rejected by the trustees who felt the archdiocese was attempting to seize their assets and possibly close the parish, hence they broke away from the Roman Catholic Church.

German bishops have approved the Blessing of Gay Unions against Vatican directions and teachings. Dr. David Ayers conducted a study entitled "Young American Catholics and the Normalization of Lesbian and Gay Sexuality."[2] This study basically says that young people are increasingly rejecting the Church's teaching on gender questions, though one might wonder if they have ever been properly catechized on the subject. Most religion teachers do not savor teaching units on any aspect of human sexuality as the Church's voice is drowned out by popular culture, the media, and entertainers.

A 2014 Pew Study declared "Young Catholics Overwhelmingly Accepting of Homosexuality"[3] and showed that many Catholics believe homosexuality should be accepted and there was a growing number of Catholics who approved of same-sex marriage, though when this data is disaggregated according to those who regularly attend Mass, there is more correlation of those attending Mass with acceptance of Church teaching.

In recent years, several Catholic schools have had to face painful decisions when a gay or lesbian teacher decides to marry publicly. Some schools have dismissed the employee, churning up vitriol and anger in their community and beyond. If there were families and students supportive of the school's decision, often they were bullied into silence by public opinion.

If a school has retained such an employee, the sponsoring religious community and/or bishop has reacted in various ways, pleasing no one. Recently St. Procopius Abbey in Lisle, Illinois announced withdrawing its sponsorship and affiliation of Benet Academy after the school hired, fired, and rehired a coach in a same-sex marriage. The school said that it maintains its Catholic identity and Benedictine mission.

A curious situation arose in Indianapolis in 2019, when the marriage of a gay couple came to the attention of the bishop and he asked the two private schools each to dismiss the men; both men taught at private high schools; one was sponsored by the Holy Cross Brothers and the other by the Jesuits. The man at Holy Cross was dismissed and the one at Brebeuf Jesuit was retained.

The bishop threatened withdrawing the Catholic identity from the schools if they did not comply. The Brebeuf situation was appealed to Rome and is on a desk somewhere in the Vatican collecting dust; however, the recent document from the Vatican *The Identity of Catholic Schools for a Culture of Dialogue* (2022) may tip the resolution towards the bishop's corner; it strongly affirms the leadership of the local bishop in deciding such matters.

With so many contradictory voices whirling in the Church on this topic, it is hard to imagine where it will all end, but it will continue to be a neuralgic issue for Catholic schools. How much scorn and venom school leaders will be able to stomach when tough decisions are reached is anyone's guess, but the pain inflicted by highly organized groups is considerable.

Perhaps the reception, i.e., widespread rejection or indifference toward *Humanae Vitae* in 1968, is the default attitude towards proclamations from Rome. Even more shocking is the abysmal ignorance about the Eucharist.

A 2019 Pew Research Poll found that 7 out of 10 Catholics believe that the bread and wine used at Communion is only symbolic.[4] Even if Catholics do not fully understand the Eucharistic teachings, one would hope that they can assent to this cherished belief. This statistic is sobering and has not been a controversial point since the Protestant Reformation.

Post–Vatican II catechesis is often lampooned and characterized as making felt and burlap banners, singing Kumbaya, and sitting on the floor for coffee table Masses with a cool priest, but if these were the seeds of aggiornamento, one must wonder about the results half a century past Vatican II.

One can also consider the arguments on worthy reception of the Eucharist and many Catholic elected officials and their insatiable appetite for supporting, funding, and celebrating abortion for all nine months of gestation. Some say these representatives should consider investing in asbestos coffins. Other Catholic writers and figures defend these figures with astonishing gymnastic arguments, becoming useful stooges and apostles for the Culture of Death, articulated by St. John Paul II's encyclical *Evangelium Vitae*. Families have definite views and opinions on these and many other topics and often enough, such families are in direct conflict with official Church teaching, and they are not happy when a school presents sound doctrine.

It is rather curious that many of the neuralgic points that dissenting Catholics have with the Roman Catholic Church, are from the same people who would be quite happy in the Episcopalian Church. We can think of theology as all that is proposed and taught about God (there is one God, there are many gods, etc.). Religion is what has been revealed to a community, culture, or people (God revealed Himself as expressed in the Nicene Creed). Belief is what an individual embraces to be true, having considered all that is proposed.

Clearly, many infants are brought into a faith community, but somewhere along life's journey, they must ratify that baptism and faith that has been handed to them. However, as is seen with many former Catholics, many just drift away, or the faith was never really cultivated. Jesus described this phenomenon in Matthew 13: 1–23 with the Parable of the Sower. The history of Arianism in the fourth century might offer a consoling message to believers who are dismayed about the ignorance of the faith.

The widespread heresy of Arianism in the early fourth century denied the divinity of Christ. Jesus was the holiest man in all of history and one should follow his teachings and live by them. However, he was not God. The Council of Nicea in 325 settled the heresy and produced the Creed that is now recited on Sundays; note the preponderance of affirmations about the Second Person of the Holy Trinity and His nature.

Arius, the founder and promoter of this belief, was arguing for its validity at the Council. St. Nicholas was there and was so outraged that he slapped Arius across the face for his utter stupidity. The believing people had accepted this error to be true. Years later, Saint Jerome commented: "The whole world groaned, and was astonished to find itself Arian." In our democratic society, there is a wide belief that whatever the majority holds is true and/or the proper direction to go.

However, the complete story of Arianism illustrates that entire groups of good-willed people can be wrong. Thankfully, Christ established in His Church, the Magisterium, to guide people through perilous times of unbelief or false teachings. The assumption that Catholics shared a common set of beliefs undergirded the Church that launched the significant expansion of Catholic schools in nineteenth century.

In the United States and particularly in urban areas, Catholic schools were seen as top priority projects to assist parents in their roles as primary educators. As noted in chapter 1, the Third Plenary Council of Baltimore in 1884 mandated that a school should be established in every parish.

> Title vi, Of the Education of Catholic Youth, treats of (i) Catholic schools, especially parochial, viz., of their absolute necessity and the obligation of pastors to establish them. Parents must send their children to such schools unless the bishop should judge the reason for sending them elsewhere to be sufficient. Ways and means are also considered for making the parochial schools more efficient. It is desirable that these schools be free. (ii) Every effort must be made to have suitable schools of higher education for Catholic youth.

Famine, poverty, and political upheaval in nineteenth-century Europe sparked waves of immigration to the United States. Often enough, these groups had little formal education. The clergy and religious who also migrated were the educated ones within the ethnic circles and it became perfectly clear to these immigrants that to advance in this new world, an education would be essential. It would seem that all the stars and planets were aligned to help form this widespread parochial school system.

The bishops charted the goal for pastors to implement with their eager and appreciative people who made monumental personal and monetary sacrifices to build the schools. Religious orders of sisters, brothers, and priests were growing in sheer numbers as a workforce and developing strong reputations for being excellent educators, and immersed themselves in staffing these schools. Clearly, parents saw these schools as excellent partners to cultivate and enshrine their Catholic faith that would permeate the entire curriculum and school day. But this partnership has grown fragile on many levels.

As previously described, there are a variety of Catholic schools. The parish elementary, and more rarely, the parish high school, are quite visible. There are private Catholic elementary schools sponsored by a religious order or with historical ties to such. There are diocesan high schools that are supported by the diocese, and there are private high schools with sponsorship or an affiliation with a religious order. All these schools serve under the leadership of the bishop and at his pleasure. One cannot ignore the growing Catholic home-schooling movement which is showing promising results.

When Catholic home-schooling began, many dismissed it, criticized it, and harbored suspicions about it. The families who were attracted to this model were devout Catholics and were determined to see that their children received a faith-filled education. Often, several like-minded families joined forces to provide the various programs. Many resources have been developed to assist the parents who choose this path.

It is not untypical that when a child arrives at middle school age, the child might transfer to a parish school, or more than likely, they will transfer to a Catholic high school that meets a family's preferences after a student completes eighth grade. Clearly, this model takes a tremendous commitment and an equal amount of ingenuity to make it work, but as was noted, there are many resources for families who wish to adopt this model (Clare 2022).

A final Catholic school configuration that is on the uptick is the Regional School. It is an increasingly rare parish that can sustain its own elementary school without some aid from a diocese or special fund to assist with operations. A Regional School is one that serves multiple parishes or a geographic area, as the name implies. Too often by attrition, because of lack of students and/or resources, a school might merge with a neighboring parish school. With better strategic planning, dioceses can better pinpoint the optimal development for a Regional School. Many considerations go into these schools.

Which parish or school has the greater promise for enrollment? What facility is in better condition? What is the leadership like at the schools? Which school has a better academic record? Are there pastors who are supportive of the Regional School and eager to help it? Or are the priests looking forward to unloading it by pulling the plug on an existing school and campus?

Sometimes, leasing the building provides a nice additional revenue stream for other projects and parish needs. In the end, a Regional School can be a stepchild that none of the sponsoring parishes are all that interested in helping.

When a school has its ties cut with one specific parish, it is difficult to engage the other sponsoring parishes. If the newly reconfigured school campus lands on the campus of a particular parish, it basically becomes the responsibility of that parish. Depending upon how the diocesan office structures responsibilities, the school building is usually seen as an asset of that specific parish.

Hence, problems with the building, such as a roof replacement or plumbing problems, may land on the desk of that parish in a greater way. The pastoral services will become the work of those priests or the priest at that parish. Even though the other representative parishes have some responsibilities, it rarely works out in a fair or harmonious plan.

Neighboring parish priests may be quite happy to let Masses, confessions, and pastoral visits slide to the man who is nearest, and that man may not be a big fan or advocate of the school. When schools are untethered from a parish, it becomes a challenge to deliver the spiritual services that define a Catholic institution. These schools can suffer from a dynamic to being "everyone's parish school, to no one's parish school." This is not good for the overall health of the school.

Private Catholic elementary and secondary schools, historically sponsored by orders of women religious and orders of brothers, also face challenges in providing the sacraments. A private Catholic high school with no priest(s) assigned to it, will turn to the parish where it is located for help. Like nursing homes and hospitals within a specific parish, that specific parish has the primary sacramental responsibilities for covering ministry to the sick there, unless in rarer cases, that there might be a priest on the staff. One priest, who had been accustomed to having at least two other priests in his parishes, now found himself in a parish alone with three large hospitals within the boundaries and no priests assigned as hospital chaplains.

With no consultation, he sent out pagers to all the neighboring priests along with a schedule of when they would be on call. The command was met with incredulity, and one priest promptly tossed the schedule and pager into the trash. Almost every parish has hidden institutions that place demands on the priests.

As the number of parish priests has diminished over the years, so too has the easy availability to assist with Mass and confessions at these private schools, especially if there is a parish elementary school of their own to tend as well. In the not-too-distant past, a parish might have had three or four priests and it would be quite simple to assign one priest as a chaplain to the school or to have a manageable rotation.

Now that curates have become fewer and their tenure as associate pastors (aka Parochial Vicars) before becoming pastors has become shorter, the pastor may be the only priest in a parish. Even though the numbers of churchgoers are falling precipitously, many of the demands are the same: a daily Mass, funerals, visiting the sick, supervising and supporting all of the ministries in a parish from the Altar Society to the St. Vincent DePaul Society, or as was popularly phrased "ministry from womb to tomb!"

The future seems to suggest that these private schools may have to incorporate the ministry of deacons more and allow the laity to lead Communion Services. This may also signal a drift from the affiliation with the Catholic church, and this may suit some boards as just fine. It is not necessarily a better scenario in many of the schools that are sponsored by orders with priests. With the diminishment of vocations, the clerical pipeline to the high schools is quickly drying up.

If a school has two or three able-bodied priests, they are quite fortunate. However, those two or three men may have full-time jobs as administrators and/or teachers, which does not make it easy for them to leave behind their regular duties to cover Advent or Lenten confessions all day for several days. These orders also rely upon the goodness of parish priests and other orders to help cover the sacraments when offered, just as the parishes request assistance from the orders.

As the future unfolds, many reports and studies describe in the US Church a confluence of fewer people attending Mass, fewer couples choosing to celebrate the sacrament of marriage, few baptisms, the closures of Catholic schools, and the diminishing number of Catholic institutions.

In 2020 Monsignor James Shea, the President of the University of Mary (Bismarck, ND), published a book entitled *From Christendom to Apostolic Mission: Pastoral Strategies for an Apostolic Age*.[5] In it, he describes Christendom as a mindset of shared assumptions and attitudes toward society where the beliefs of Christianity are a given and accepted way of being.

Christendom was noted for its many institutions and missions to nurture committed disciples, heal the sick, and educate men and women for lives of faith and service. As in Europe, the United States can safely say that Christendom's day has passed. As noted earlier, but it is worth repeating, decades before he became Pope Benedict XVI, Cardinal Joseph Ratzinger also saw this day when he prognosticated the near future of the Church and its diminishment.

> As a small society, [the Church] will make much bigger demands on the initiative of her individual members. . . . It will be hard going for the Church, for the process of crystallization and clarification will cost her much valuable energy. It will make her poor and cause her to become the Church of the meek. . . . The process will be long and wearisome as was the road from the false progressivism on the eve of the French Revolution—when a bishop might be thought smart if he made fun of dogmas and even insinuated that the existence of God was by no means certain. . . . But when the trial of this sifting is past, a great power will flow from a more spiritualized and simplified Church. (Ratzinger 1969)

Simply put, one must wonder about the future of Catholic schools as the crown jewel of the Catholic Church in the United States. There is no doubt that such schools will have an important role to play in the future of the Church's educational mission. With the demise of government schools, the reliable service of Catholic schools will remain an attractive alternative to weary parents.

The nerves of parents are wearing thin as the public schools seem to be in constant losing battles with powerful teacher unions; this has been especially difficult in large urban areas. However, parents using the government system will have even less influence on their child's spiritual formation. This is particularly true for teens in high school and possibly after First Confession and First Communion catechesis.

Shea points to the rapid and sad collapse of the Church in Quebec, Belgium, Spain, and Ireland. He notes that the Catholic culture seemed secure while a secular world was busy undermining the faith. As he wisely observed:

> Almost overnight, these societies went from being strongly Catholic to aggressively secular. One reason for the rapid collapse was the overarching vision of the society had been changing over a course of time, but the change was not perceived, and the institutions of the Church were not adjusting to it; they rather continued to be led under an attitude of "business as usual." At a certain point, the eroding Christian vision could no longer bear the weight of the culture; the house collapsed, and great was its fall. These admittedly complex situations point to a working principle: institutional and ecclesiastical strategies that are suited to Christendom do not work well in an apostolic setting. (Shea 2020)

Monsignor Shea contrasts that the Church currently finds itself in a period more akin to the apostolic era.

In an apostolic age, the Church is in a sense self-conscious. Christians know by daily experience that they inhabit a spiritual and moral world different from and often in opposition to the one around them, and that demands a greater sense of their distinct call. The various benefits that accrue in a Christendom culture are not present. Error in all its forms, doctrinal and moral, is rife. In such a cultural atmosphere it can be difficult for Christians to sustain their own spiritual and moral vision. Material advantages are offered to those who make peace with the non-Christian majority, and the attractiveness of the ruling vision is hard to resist, especially for the most vulnerable. Among other problems, it becomes more difficult to raise children in the faith.

For those who think that the current crises facing the Church are insurmountable, they do not know their history. The study of Church history is one of the most consoling endeavors one can engage in. Those early three centuries are filled with bewildering odds that do not favor the little movement that started on the first Easter Sunday. Bishop N. T. Wright composed a scholarly and painstaking biography of the Apostle Paul.

Paul's mission to the Gentiles and world shows all the hard decisions, rejections, and starting everything from scratch. While this current era still has a significant number of institutions established, keeping them afloat will be especially challenging. If the prospect of government funding materializes, what strings will be attached, or what encroachments will be launched?

Will the Church's consistent teaching about marriage and sexuality be firewalls that prevent the flow of funding? How elastic will a diocese and its schools be with the increasingly adversarial world? One can be assured that there will be watchdogs prepared to litigate any suspicions.

In the future, Catholic schools will have a challenging time in maintaining their religious identity and purpose. A popular term that emerged in the days following Vatican II and the promulgation of the encyclical *Humane Vitae*, was that of Cafeteria Catholics; those people who identified their membership in the Catholic church but felt comfortable to pick and choose what teachings suited them and leaving behind those that did not fit well with their worldview.

This term certainly predated the more common declaration that "one is spiritual but not religious," showing a connection with a transcendent reality but without being burdened with belonging to a community or adhering to any beliefs or principles. A "make it up as you go" spirituality stands outside the reality that is Christianity's original Church that includes Revelation, i.e., that which God has disclosed to the world through Sacred Scripture, Tradition, and the Magisterium.

So, in response to the claim expressed in the chapter's title, "I Thought that This Was Supposed to Be a Catholic School," there will be many definitions of what that means. If a school is striving to honor the teachings and mission of the Church, the administration and faculty may get crossways with some families. However, such a school will hopefully attract families that are searching for such a school that can share in the formation of their sons and daughters in such a manner.

Some families will tolerate things they do not agree with, such as frequent reminders about honoring the Sunday Mass obligation, but others will want to exploit aspects of the Church to their advantage and view. Catholics who support abortion rights might claim that the Church is a misogynist organization that should focus on forgiveness and supporting choice. Advocates of students confused with gender dysphoria will protest when special accommodations are not made, that the school is not a welcoming institution as Jesus would want it to be.

Catholic high schools will face cases around the transgender issue. A biological female will identify as male and wants to attend an all-male school or a boy wants to attend an all-girls school. If the school has been waffling on various gender issues, it will certainly get entangled in this web. Pope Francis and the teachings of the Church all accept and promulgate the biological facts that science teaches around this issue, namely that hormones and surgery cannot erase the DNA, and gift from God the Creator.

Given the investment that a Catholic education entails, all parents should be wise consumers. Non-Catholic families often appreciate the caliber of education found in Catholic schools and the discipline, safety, and spiritual atmosphere, but one that does not proselytize or make any demands they might find offensive.

Perhaps this attitude represents many Catholic families as well who are attracted more to the sound education and respectful environment. Given the diverse voices found in the Church today, what a Catholic school is and/or should be is something that is debated. In the popular imagination, Catholic schools are still staffed by nuns wearing their full habits, but that day has passed.

When considering the long-term viability of Catholic schools, one can wonder if any school will operate in ten, twenty, thirty, or fifty years from now. Given the grim statistics of plummeting numbers of churchgoers and smaller families with fewer parents seeking baptism, it would seem that the schools make up a valuable project from the culture of Christendom, but how will they be able to reinvent themselves in this apostolic age meaningfully?

Or will the schools simply adapt to what the market demands and water down the Catholic identity to a Catholic Lite culture? Ultimately, this is a question of a disconnect between an attitude of evangelizing and providing a solid education.

When Catholic institutions diminish or cancel the goal of making disciples and/or deepening the faith and commitment of the community, the project is compromised. Sadly, this is most readily seen in Catholic higher education.

Established to educate the laity, a goal was infused to turn out well-informed active members of the Church. Vatican II certainly championed this position in describing the role of the laity to be a leaven in society not to make a theocracy but to bring the joy of the Gospel to the world. Sadly, for those public figures who identify as Catholic to some degree, they have been severe disappointments on so many pivotal moral issues.

As noted previously, it would be a rare document on Catholic schools that does not cite that parents are the primary educators of their children, and schools assist the families in this role. When the home and school are on the same page regarding faith formation, academics, and discipline, a strong culture is clear and is characterized by mutual respect. When families are on a different page from the school, trouble is not far behind, especially when students commit misdemeanors which are a part of growing up and to be expected.

Much has been written about the changing dispositions of problematic parents and the names convey the force of nature aimed at the school: Tiger Moms, Lawnmower Parents, Snowplow Parents, Helicopter Parenting, Velcro Parents are among the current genres. While these cast a dark picture in some ways, most administrators would attest that you spend about 90 percent of your time dealing with 10 percent of the population in a school community and are grateful for that ratio.

KEY IDEAS IN CHAPTER 2

- Dealing with difficult parents
- Students who get into serious trouble
- Drifting from the Catholic mission
- Why families choose a Catholic school
- Nonobservant Catholics
- Some ways that Covid-19 impacted the Church and schools
- Rejection of core teachings and beliefs
- LGBTQ teachings and issues
- Different kinds of Catholic schools: Parochial, Private, Consolidated, Regional
- From Christendom to Apostolic Mission, need for a new mindset of evangelization

NOTES

1. Dreher, R. 2017
2. Ayers, D. 2021
3. Lipka, M. 2014
4. Smith, G. 2019
5. Shea, M. 2020

Chapter 3

"We Hire for Mission and We Fire for Mission"

Easier Said than Done!

"We Hire for Mission and We Fire for Mission." This is a catch phrase one often hears in Leadership Classes and at big meetings held by Catholic institutions. Sounds strong and responsible, does it not? Hiring can be a long and arduous process but compared to dismissing a problem and/or under-performing employee, it is the easier of the two processes.

The court of public opinion is quick to crucify school leaders who make mission-based employment decisions that result in termination or non-renewal of a contract of a faculty or staff member. Typically, teacher contracts and other contracts are at will; that is, the contract is good for one year.

Some high schools and perhaps some private Catholic elementary schools foolishly offered tenure to faculty, which makes no sense given the history of tenure and its shaky future even in higher education where it was once and continues to be firmly ensconced. Faculty see it as an inviable guarantee for continuation of employment despite mediocre or poor performance after tenure being granted.

Generally, schools can dismiss employees (even with tenure) but it will not be a simple or easy exercise outside of some of the most egregious cases. Perhaps the best interpretation one could put on tenure for K–12 faculty would be that they are entrusted with the mission of the school and are seen as senior partners in the school and are regarded as a trusted leader. Unfortunately, some tenure candidates just completed the required number of years of service to slip by and then they can begin coasting.

Sometimes the school's mission has been compromised to have a teacher in front of the classroom for many understandable reasons. The hiring process follows a fairly routine calendar. In late winter or very early in the second semester, non-binding "Letters of Intent" go out to faculty to solicit their intention about returning for the coming academic year.

This helps for planning if a faculty member is moving to a different city, changing careers, changing schools, or retiring. If a faculty member is planning to return and various protocols and needs of the school are met, a contract will be offered. Before the end of the current school year, the contract is signed by said faculty/staff member as well as the school leadership. Now the school has the assurance that a position will be covered as the school sails into the summer months.

For those not returning, the school has been afforded time in the late winter and early spring to advertise the position and fill it, both of which are very time-consuming for the principal and his/her staff. As the school year winds down, the principal hopes that the coming school year is covered. When school recesses for summer, people are taking vacations and many offices have a slower pace, so one hopes that the workforce is set and tied up with a pretty bow.

Just when all seems to be in order for a smooth beginning to the new school year, unpleasant employment surprises are not uncommon. It would be a rare year that a principal has not been dealt a major-league employment headache on the doorstep of opening school.

Imagine a week before faculty orientation in early August when a teacher decides to break his or her contract—Surprise! It happens all the time. Imagine if the school told a faculty member that their services would not be needed a week before the launch of the school year? It would be front page news; in fact, it has been front page news, unfortunately.

Yet, this is not an untypical scenario, and usually it involves a position that is very difficult to fill such as in Math or Science, but the other departments are well-represented by faculty who deliver a last-minute stink bomb and there is really very little the school can do about the contract despite the legal checks and balances. Schools are reticent to pursue a legal reprimand and, sadly, unscrupulous school leaders sometimes poach employees.

The administration is supposed to be understanding and forgiving for the most frivolous reasons; often, people are heading to a suburban government school for a higher salary, or they might change careers. Catholic school principals with high standards always ask if a late-applying potential candidate is under contract somewhere else. If they are, the principal will probably stop the hiring process out of respect for the other school and a value of not doing unto others what you yourself would dislike, even given an urgent need.

There can be cases when circumstances make sense for the abrupt change, but courtesy phone calls are of the utmost importance. None of these moves toward breaking a contract are terrible decisions, but the timing is horrendous. Ask any principal about such August surprises.

In advertising a position at a Catholic school, how does the language reflect the mission of the school? Is it specific in stating that the school desires a practicing Catholic? If the advertisement is not specific about such a reality, a school is on a fishing trip, and they may not get what they truly desire.

Many Catholic schools have fine leaders who are not Catholic and are very supportive of the mission; in fact, sometimes these folks are more committed than some of the non-practicing Catholics who are on a faculty. It is not unusual for a school's administration to find themselves in a compromising situation driven by desperation to fill a vacant position. So, the mission may be compromised to get a competent teacher and qualified teacher into the classroom, and maybe not.

Just because someone claims to be Catholic does not assure a vibrant member of the flock; a mouse might be born in a cookie jar, but that does not make the mouse a cookie. In fact, non-Catholics have made wonderful contributions to the Catholic school project over the years, bringing their experience and worldview to enrich the community. What is essential is that such colleagues understand the mission of the school and are always supportive of it. It is not unusual to have such members cited for an even stronger devotion to the mission than cradle Catholics.

The University of Notre Dame has done an exemplary job of hiring practicing Catholics and setting a bar for having a critical mass of practicing Catholics. As the old Latin expression noted: *Nemo dat quod non habet* (no one gives what one does not have). Many Catholic schools are under the impression that they cannot ask about religious practices of the candidates, but they can and should. Catholic institutions have drifted into a foggy valley of trying to talk about faith but not addressing it head on.

Social justice jargon, values, etc. become the circular approach to matters of faith and spirituality. This is similar to a growing and bizarre phenomenon of going to Catholic events, especially fundraisers, and the prayer does not begin with the Sign of the Cross or mention the name of Jesus and the prayer leader even tiptoes around God.

Some think not making the Sign of the Cross or not mentioning Jesus makes non-believers feel comfortable; would these potentially offended people in turn make believers comfortable by mentioning Jesus at their events? There is no shortage of hand-wringing and watering down the faith with some misguided notion of not being offensive to people of other faith traditions or unbelievers.

Another challenging issue facing Catholic school leaders is hiring for diversity. Students, alumni, boards, and schools will often express a desire to have a faculty that reflects the composition of the student body. Again, this is easier said than done. When people speak of diversity, more often than not, they are speaking almost exclusively of racial diversity and possibly ethnic diversity (economic, geographic, religious, et al., are usually not great interest points nor do they count for those keeping score).

Sadly, people of color are not entering the education profession in great numbers. In fact, the entire profession is experiencing tremendous shortages, and the pandemic has not helped to avert this downward trend.

> Since 2010, enrollment in teacher preparation programs nationwide has declined by more than one-third, according to a new analysis from the Center for American Progress, meaning approximately 340,000 fewer students are enrolled in teacher preparation programs today. Along with Oklahoma, Michigan, Pennsylvania, Delaware, Illinois, Idaho, Indiana, New Mexico, and Rhode Island all notched enrollment declines of 50%. And in nine states—California, Illinois, Indiana, Michigan, New Jersey, New York, Ohio, Oklahoma, and Pennsylvania—enrollment dropped by more than 10,000 students. . . . Perhaps most alarming, when researchers disaggregated the enrollment data by race, they found that the number of black and Latino students enrolled in teacher preparation programs had decreased by 25%. The teacher workforce, in which 80% of educators are white, 9% are Latino and 7% are black, is already less racially diverse than the overall U.S. labor force, despite being a profession in which the importance of teachers of color cannot be overstated.
>
> Recent research has shown that for black children, having just one black teacher in elementary school are more likely to graduate and more likely to enroll in college. But teacher preparation programs enrolled nearly 15,000 fewer black students in 2018 than in 2010.[1]

As discouraging as these numbers are in general, they do not paint a rosy picture for Catholic schools. While some teachers might be attracted to teaching in a Catholic school, higher salaries and geography will usually draw away an excellent candidate. Catholic schools strive to approximate the salary and benefits of a government-run school, but those realities usually fall short by comparison.

There are some intangible benefits, such as actually being able to teach and not face unending discipline problems. One English teacher who switched from a government/public high school to a Catholic high school claimed that the culture took some getting used to. He was accustomed to a police officer posted outside his classroom and roaming the halls breaking up fights and addressing various disturbances.

Many Schools of Education are experiencing a drop in enrollment. The earning power of an education degree and career in education is sufficient for a good life but will not be as attractive when compared to other professions. With a dropping pool of possible teacher candidates, it becomes even harder to find those candidates who will put the mission of the school as a primary attractor. Frankly, highly qualified minority candidates in the field of education will have far more options as they survey the job markets because they are so enthusiastically sought.

Again, this is an easier request/demand to make than it is to fulfill, despite the best of intentions and efforts. Many enthusiastic and supportive administrators are simply told that they ". . . did not try hard enough, nor are they looking in the right places." A good response would be to ask the critics to please recommend and direct qualified people to the hiring portal.

When being interviewed for positions, potential faculty and staff should be thoroughly vetted about the Catholic mission of the school. They should be asked: 1. How do you understand the Catholic mission of the school? 2. What excites you about the mission? 3. How do you see yourself contributing to the mission? 4. Is there anything in the mission that you would find problematic?

It would also be useful to require a candidate to submit a letter of recommendation from his or her pastor; this is typical in Catholic elementary schools but not as prevalent in high schools, which is a missed opportunity that can backfire on a school; what gets measured gets done.

Some might object or quibble as to how one would define a practicing Catholic. At the very minimum, the person should be a registered and contributing member of a parish faith community. These are at least verifiable markers. The person does not have to be a fishing buddy with the pastor, but there should be some engagement in the life of a parish, like showing up each Sunday for Mass.

Such evidence will be helpful in finding not only a competent teacher but someone who wishes to be a role model for the students. Glossing over such questions can lead to all kinds of hiring disasters. It is good to presume the best in people, but as President Ronald Reagan advised: "Trust but verify."

It is not unheard of that after a teacher has been hired, unsavory things are discovered about the person. A teacher cohabitating with their partner with no intention of marrying. Views supporting abortion which are expressed to a class. Endorsing contrary attitudes with the Church over same-sex attraction. Expressing condescending thoughts about the Church's beliefs regarding divorce and remarriage, women's ordination, and other perspectives that are at odds with official teachings of the Church can come into the light of day.

Of course, there are sufficient voices from clergy, religious, and lay leaders with no unpublished thoughts promoting dissenting views on such topics and undermining many settled questions. As a wise professor once said, "For every heresy, there is a fool to maintain it."

Principals will receive a phone call or more frequently emails complaining about a spurious view that a faculty member may have expressed or commented upon that is divergent from Church teachings. This launches a troubling situation, especially in a high school or elementary school. Institutions of Catholic higher education can discuss thorny issues, but even there, the answers to settled questions do not change.

Imagine a religion teacher who is personally Pro-Choice on the abortion issue. This teacher keeps these views to herself, but one day made a disparaging remark about a statement by the bishop supporting the March for Life in Washington. A student whose family is very involved in supporting the Pro-Life movement was upset by the comment but did not want to confront the teacher. This student went home and told his parents, who contacted the principal of the school.

Typically, the school administrator will ask if the student understood the teacher correctly. Did the student have a respectful conversation with the teacher about the issue? Did the parent contact the teacher? Students can be reticent to confront or contradict a teacher for fear of grade reprisals, and parents are equally hesitant to go to the source because they do not want their son's or daughter's relationship with the teacher to sour. So, the concern is sent to a vice principal, or to the principal.

The parent usually wants this school leader to investigate the matter under a cloak of mystery, since no names are supposed to be mentioned because of a desire not to make waves. This is not a calm situation for the teacher since there is no context for the concern or identity of the accuser. During the course of a school day and in a class, many things are said by a teacher, and it would be very easy to be quoted out of context by a dozing student. However, sometimes, the concern is spot on and needs to be addressed by the school's leadership.

Leadership will always encourage the aggrieved parent to go directly to the teacher or coach and try to work things out to everyone's satisfaction on the levels closest to the issue. It is good to have higher levels of responsiveness, if necessary, but if a problem can be handled on its lowest level, it is all the better.

This theory of subsidiarity permeates the Church and serves everyone better since those most closely involved in a concern have a better understanding of the matter. An example would be wanting to change the mascot at a school; you would not attempt to drag the pope or bishop into the conversation, but one would address it most locally among those concerned at the school, i.e., current families, alumni, the PTA, the board, and administration.

Catholic school teachers' contracts include a ministerial or mission clause. The Supreme Court Case of *Hosanna-Tabor Evangelical Lutheran Church and School v. Equal Employment Opportunity Commission* (2012) established that federal discrimination laws do not apply to religious organizations and those they choose to hire as religious leaders. Religious schools began to designate teachers as ministers, giving the school greater latitude in dismissing problematic faculty. When contracts were changed to adopt this language, many faculty bristled.

Saint Ignatius College Prep in Chicago developed the following language for a teacher's contract, that while not designating a teacher as a minister, still holds the teacher as a spiritual role model in the first section under the Teacher's Duties:

> Spiritual Development and Serving as a Role Model. Faculty Member agrees to contribute to the Catholic, Jesuit mission of the School, which includes the integration of Catholic beliefs and teachings in all teaching and programming as described in the JSN document What Makes a Jesuit School Jesuit. The School considers each Faculty Member an essential ambassador and partner of its spiritual mission, who agrees to integrate spiritual principles with teaching within his or her academic discipline or co-curricular activity, as appropriate.
>
> Faculty Member shall teach and act consistently as an adult role model and representative of the School's mission, in accordance with the stated philosophy, attitudes, objectives, and policies of the School, as defined in the Faculty Handbook and as described in the Saint Ignatius Profile of an Ignatian Educator. Faculty Member agrees to consistently support, teach, and comport himself/ herself in accordance with Catholic beliefs and values.

Diocesan contracts for elementary and secondary schools, as well as other private schools, would probably reflect language such as this to varying degrees. A few years ago, a young teacher had shared with her class that she had recently been engaged. Of course, the high school students were very interested in how the couple met, etc. While one's personal life is bound to enter the classroom, a teacher must always be discreet and judicious in what is shared with the students.

Some students wanted to know where she and her fiancé were living; the assumption being that, like just about everyone else, she was cohabitating with the man. The teacher was a devout and practicing Catholic. She took this opportunity to speak about the wisdom and teaching of the Church around the Sacrament of Marriage and how they were honoring those beliefs and that she and her fiancé were not sharing a home.

This teacher was fulfilling the spirit of the contract. However, it is easy to imagine a contrary situation where the teacher's personal and public life are undermining the very values being promoted by the school. Within the contract, there are remedies to dismiss a problematic faculty member. These are fairly standard reasons for cause. Again, the contract language from Saint Ignatius College Prep serves as a template:

"Termination During the Term. The School may terminate this Contract during the Term at the discretion of the School, effective as of a date determined by the School (including immediately and including without advance notice), including for the following reasons:

1. conduct or teaching contrary to (1) the School's expectations as stated in the Saint Ignatius Profile of an Ignatian Educator, (2) the Faculty Handbook, (3) other directives given by the School;
2. unsatisfactory performance, including incompetence, insubordination, neglect of duties, or unexcused absences;
3. illegal, immoral, unethical, fraudulent, or dishonest conduct on or off the job and including conduct prior to the Term that is learned of during the Term;
4. the inability of Faculty Member to perform the essential functions of the appointment for greater than 90 days in any rolling 12-month period, or the exhaustion of all available non-discretionary leave, paid or unpaid, under the School's policies (as determined by the Principal and/or President in consultation with the Vice-President of Finance, who shall interpret this ground so as to ensure compliance with all applicable legal requirements pertaining to disabilities and leave);
5. economic hardship, war, governmental control, fire, natural disaster, state of emergency, pandemic, act of God, or other similar events outside of the control of the School, or other event that substantially impairs or disrupts the operation of the School, as determined by the President or the Board of Trustees; and
6. a determination by the President or the Board of Trustees, in his/her/its sole discretion, that a reduction in the number of faculty is warranted due to variations in student enrollment or for other unanticipated or unexpected reasons."

The contract continues with sections on the Resolution of Disputes and the Timely Assertion of Claims. Faculty members who are dismissed or not renewed have recourse to address their situation, but a school's leadership team will only move toward termination or nonrenewal under the guidance of legal counsel and for substantive reasons.

So, when a teacher is suddenly removed or not renewed, students, parents, and the school community will most likely want to know what happened to the said teacher. Unfortunately, the school leaders are not legally nor ethically at liberty to disclose these personnel matters and ethically out of respect for the teacher who has been dismissed. What inquiring minds can easily surmise is that the person was fired for cause, i.e., one or more of those reasons listed above.

Of course, the terminated teacher may wish to publicize their grievance on social media or in the press. When this happens, the school is in a terrible position because if the facts of the case were actually known, many reasonable people would probably see the wisdom of the school, but when only one side of a story is told, that is the only version that is out for public consumption, and it is always easy to demonize institutions and school administrators.

So, when such cases make it to the press, the school can only say that they cannot say anything. It is good to remember that there are always two sides to a case. One draws strength from the image of Jesus during his trial and is led away for mocking resentment and the negative press and condemnations.

Schools can be composed of a wide range of staff and teachers who represent exceptional professionals, caring role models, to mediocre hangers-on. When hiring, one of the most important tasks to complete with prospective candidates is to pick up the phone and check out the references submitted and to contact the last place of employment. One school hired a retired priest that was superficially known to the school and was hired without checking his previous roosting place.

He seemed a suitable candidate for the alumni work for which he was hired but turned out to be a lackluster and crabby old man with little work left in him before the crack of noon. Eventually, and not too soon after being hired, he was released from his position, which was a relief to everyone. A phone call to his previous school would have averted a painful turn of events rather than relying on optics and good will.

Schools need to pick up the phone no matter how well known a candidate might be. The call will probably confirm a candidate's attractive skills, but it might also save much time and headaches if something needs to be communicated off-the-record. People often enough do not want to put a negative comment in writing because they do not want it discovered.

Hence, a letter of recommendation that has a terse and anodyne comment like the following is usually code for "something is not right": e.g., "Ms. Jackson was employed at Holy Cross Elementary from August 2017–June 2018; she had her own transportation. If I can be of further assistance, let me know," signed [the principal]. The principal will find out that Ms. Jackson usually worked four-day weeks or showed up inebriated on occasion.

Applications for open positions are interesting. A school might advertise for a fifth grade teacher. It is amazing to see the stack of applications that arrive. These submissions run the gamut from people who clearly did not read and/or understand the requirements stated in the job's posting to well-qualified applicants. Some do not have the proper degree and/or certification.

Some have credentials in totally irrelevant fields, such as Animal Husbandry or Folk Dancing. Clearly, these applications are quickly set aside in the first culling of the stack. Then there are the others which look promising.

Even among the stronger candidates, all may seem in order but upon closer investigation, the sterling application may not be all that is stated. Hyperbole and making something of nothing is not unheard of in such processes. There are many websites with suggestions on how to pad a resumé and exaggerate minor actions into amazing accomplishments.

Many favorable applicants turn out to be NOT what was submitted on paper. Principals and school leaders responsible for hiring have an enormous and serious task to vet the candidates properly and to make certain that the person is qualified for the position. This is analogous to the deceptive social media activity known as catfishing. In fact, the hiring process is among the most critical tasks for the well-being of the school's mission and its culture.

Finding the right fit is a challenge. Faculty and staff clearly have jobs to do but working in a Catholic school requires much more of its people. Will these new staff members get along with the other adults in the building? Will they treat the custodians with as much respect as they would extend to the principal or pastor? Are parents afforded proper and timely attention when concerns arise? Building a culture of collegiality is integral to the success of a school.

Faculty and staff who chronically arrive as school starts and are the first ones out of the building at the close of a school day, despite stipulations in a contract about such expectations to stay at least a half hour longer after the final bell, do not contribute to the project. Students often want to see teachers or staff after school when classes are complete at the end of a day.

Parents might want to stop by for an important conversation. If the school professionals project a surly attitude, as though these out-of-class duties are an imposition, it does not speak well of the school and is definitely not the customer service that students, colleagues, and families expect and deserve. These are not 8:00am–3:00pm jobs, these are vocations.

A college professor once made the following distinction about the difference between a vocation and a job. An undergraduate was applying to medical school and was hesitant about being a doctor. The professor proposed that the student think of all the money that medical school would cost along with all the student loans that were on the horizon.

He spoke of the rigorous curriculum and demands of being a physician in great detail so that the student's eyes were glazing over. Then he posed the following scenario. "If you were to win the Super Lottery of untold millions of dollars, in fact, so much money that you would never have to work again and live a life of unimaginable comfort and luxury, would you still want to be a physician?"

If the answer is "no," then perhaps being a doctor is not a vocation. However, if the response is a "yes," then that suggests that the desire to be a doctor is more of a calling and vocation. There is nothing wrong with having a job, but the frame of mind of one who would still invest speaks of a deep calling to be a physician. Teachers and professional staffs are certainly not going to become wealthy from their labors, but they will earn a comfortable income.

Many teachers in Catholic schools have a sense of purpose and would see their careers as a vocation. Many would describe it as a seed planted by God and nurtured along the way by effective mentors and teachers whom they encountered along the way. Most would cite generous teachers who inspired them to become teachers or school leaders. Catholic schools thrive when animated by such caring professionals, not those who are minimalists and do only what is required.

Emily Valencia serves as the Admissions Director at Ursuline Academy in St. Louis, Missouri; she had been the Director of Student Activities at Saint Ignatius College Prep in Chicago. Her extensive experience in working with student organizations and extra-curricular activities provides a useful vantage point in describing the benefits for faculty service and leadership beyond the classroom. Among the benefits for such service, she noted:

- Adults, especially novice teachers will gain confidence,
- Get to know students in a different setting,
- Take on a challenge and develop new skills,
- Integrate yourself quickly into the community,
- And make a difference while having fun. (Valencia, Emily. 2021)

Many schools require faculty to act as moderator for at least one club; depending upon the school, these sometimes have stipends attached. However, there is a range of requirements depending upon the activity.

Some student organizations meet infrequently and many fizzle out due to lack of attendance over the year, so the faculty involvement is miniscule. Other organizations take an enormous amount of time and involve travel, such as the Model United Nations, debate, or the chess club; some of these highly active organizations require full weekends. Many adults find these activities are in constant competition with other student commitments.

If a club is going to meet after school and a student has soccer or baseball practice, athletics will always take precedence. If students are involved in drama or choir, those will often take priority, though these activities are more seasonal. It is an interesting phenomenon to see how students find their niche and way of belonging in a school community through the extra-curriculars.

Retreats and days of recollection occupy a privileged place in the life of Catholic schools. Elementary schools might have a full day of prayer, service, and reflection. Catholic high schools often structure longer retreats that might include one or more overnights at a retreat center. Kairos is a well-known and widely used retreat model for juniors and seniors.

Students will speak of the powerful impact of the retreat as fellow students, faculty, and staff offer various reflections that can be religious but generally involve overcoming obstacles or painful experiences with a connection to faith. Adults can encounter many unanticipated challenges on these retreats, which will sometimes stretch their comfort zone.

The climate of the retreat strives to create a friendly and trusting environment for everyone. Rules and expectations for behavior are clearly stated to the students and their parents. As talks are given and personal information is trustingly shared, students open and reveal experiences and attitudes that can cause great concern.

Someone talks about suicide ideation or another student talks about being in therapy for a compromising relationship that might necessitate contacting Child Protective Services, would be two examples where faculty need to respond and engage the school leadership for direction. It has been known for students to have a meltdown and be removed from the retreat. Some students bring and consume marijuana, cigarettes, or alcohol, despite dire reiterations and warnings found in the school handbook. These are unpleasant discoveries for chaperones to make.

While these are infrequent episodes, when they occur, they can spoil the entire experience and hijack the retreat as the speculation on the misdemeanor and its adjudication eclipse the retreat. Some adults do not want to deal with these kinds of episodes, which are sadly part of the landscape of student formation and discipline. Faculty need to be prepared as best as possible for all imaginable problems.

The challenges of finding the right professionals for Catholic schools will be increasingly challenging. The pool of qualified professionals is getting smaller, and the trend does not seem to attract individuals to the profession, especially those candidates who are sought for diversity.

Thankfully, there are candidates who enjoy incorporating prayer and faith into their work and seeing their profession as a vocation, as described earlier. The opportunities for prayer, days of recollection, and the celebration of Mass can motivate some teachers. However, things often come down to a salary and benefits.

This is not to paint teachers and the professional staff as being greedy, but with a car lien, a mortgage, rent, their own families to educate, income is not irrelevant. Some of the private high schools will typically pay a higher salary than diocesan schools, as they would not be held to a mandated diocesan pay scale.

In some places, it was typical to have yet another pay scale for religious men and women at a much lower salary; this was presumably to help them honor their vows of poverty, but no one lost any sleep underpaying these teachers a pittance; indeed, the whole Catholic school system is indebted to these generous professionals.

Without them and their basic contributed services for decades, the schools would not have flourished as they did. Unfortunately, such thinking has landed many orders in a precarious situation with the many elderly members to care for and next to nothing in savings or endowment to provide proper health care.

Fortuitously, along with an annual collection in Advent to help these struggling orders, an organization called Support Our Aging Religious (SOAR) has emerged to help fill in the gaps for what the elderly members may need. One of the givens that religious brought to the schools was their full and active participation in the life of the Church. Herein lies the monumental challenge for administrators, that of finding qualified and teachers who are active members of their faith communities.

Being an active member of the Church is always baked into the common denominator of seeking candidates; however, as noted above, there will always be exceptions with representation of other faith traditions, and these can be most welcome as has been evident in many schools. Cultivating teachers and leadership for Catholic schools has been a focus of several Catholic universities and colleges.

> Catholic Higher Education Supporting Catholic Schools (CHESCS) is a national network of Catholic colleges and universities with professional education departments, schools, divisions, and centers directly affiliated with NCEA [National Catholic Educational Association] to enhance P-12 Catholic schools for the good of society and the good of the Catholic Church. CHESCS brings together resources and influence of Catholic institutions of higher education to partner with and strengthen P-12 Catholic schooling through research, teaching and leadership programs, professional development, and advocacy. (2021)

These programs have their work cut out for them. With the number of Catholic schools declining, many of the candidates may wonder what is the advantage of investing in a degree program for a system that is downsizing. Many major archdioceses have launched programs to merge parishes, schools, and other institutions to save resources and better position leadership opportunities.

The Archdiocese of New York has *Making All Things New*, the Archdiocese of Chicago has *Renew My Church*, the Archdiocese of Detroit has *Unleash the Gospel*, and the Archdiocese of St. Louis has *All Things New*; while these efforts have upbeat titles, their work faces the painful reality of maximizing the diminishing resources of priest personnel, aging parish facilities with neglected and deferred maintenance in desperate need of attention but no funding streams, and more empty pews for Sunday Mass.

Despite the sincere and necessary efforts to bring people along with these closures and consolidations and how much better things will be, many of the faithful who have invested time, treasure, and talent have the attitude towards these programs best expressed in the title of Judge Judy's best seller—*Don't Pee on My Leg and Tell Me It's Raining*. In many of these parishes that are marching toward the guillotine, the school had been closed years before and was perhaps the canary in the mine shaft foretelling a declining future.

As neighborhoods change in large urban areas, people move to suburban areas with excellent government/public schools. Historically, when the Catholic elementary school's enrollment started dropping, it often coincided with the exit of religious women who staffed the schools, because of their own preferences, declining numbers, and aging workforce.

Next were the increasing financial budgets, which necessitated diverting almost every resource of the parish into the school to serve a shrinking number of families. Then, if possible, such schools would see if there were options to consolidate with neighboring parishes and establish regional schools. Hence, the forecast for growth and vitality are very limited and encouraging people to get specific degrees for serving in Catholic schools will be challenging.

As leadership within dioceses and those religious communities that still sponsor schools grapple with these many stresses and challenges, one remaining constant is the need for talented and committed leadership. Identifying candidates and cultivating them will be a challenge. The Catholic universities mentioned above with CHESCS typically offer a reduction in tuition and that is frequently met by a diocesan subsidy, so institutions will invest in people.

Catholic school leaders in these programs will make a smaller tuition investment than their peers preparing for careers in government schools. These programs can serve the greater question of this chapter in finding the right people who will bring a zeal for their faith to the students and communities that they serve.

KEY IDEAS IN CHAPTER 3

- Hiring Practices
- Termination and Nonrenewal of Contracts
- Public Outcry over Nonrenewal
- Termination for Cause
- The Need for Practicing Catholics
- The Precipitous Drop in Schools of Education with Teacher Preparation Programs
- Hiring for Diversity
- Hiring for Mission Questions and Procedures
- Examples of Faculty Undermining the Mission

- Teacher Contracts Examples
- Teaching as a Vocation, Not a 8:00–3:00 Job
- The Importance of Student Activities and Extra-Curriculars
- Pay Scales for Religious
- Catholic Higher Education Supporting Catholic Schools (CHESCS)
- Diocesan Downsizing Initiatives: Implications for Catholic Schools

NOTES

1. Camera 2019

Chapter 4

Religious Communities
Absentee Landlords

In the first half of the twentieth century and leading up to Vatican II, and in a few years afterwards, most urban parishes were distinguished by four prominent buildings: the church, the school, the rectory, and the convent. Many of the parish elementary schools were staffed by women religious with four, six, or more sisters providing leadership in the principal's office and the backbone of the faculty.

High schools were either diocesan, i.e., operated and supported by the diocese often with the help of religious communities, or they were private schools owned and operated by various religious communities like the Sisters of St. Joseph of Carondelet, the Society of Mary, or the LaSallian Christian Brothers. All these schools come under the jurisdiction of the local bishop, while the governance model of the private schools gave them greater latitude in administration. However, there was no financial support from the local church.

The religious communities infused all these schools with their charism, traditions, and educational philosophies. People took a great deal of pride in having been taught by a particular order. Even though most communities do not have a "third order" or organization where the laity can have a special affiliation with a religious congregation by being enrolled in a spiritual relationship, (not legal or binding), many alumni would manifest a devotion and affection for the women and men who taught them.

"*I was taught by the Irish Christian Brothers in high school.*" "*The Dominican Sisters from Mission San Jose ran our grade school.*" "*I had the Sisters of Mercy throughout grade school and high school.*" Such declarations as these have gone the way of the maniple.

With rare exceptions, most Catholic schools are staffed almost entirely by lay men and women. NCEA noted that in 2021–2022 the combination of sisters, brothers, and clergy represented 2.6 percent of the workforce in Catholic elementary and secondary schools combined. Even today, one reads or hears about someone being educated by the Jesuits, or they received a Jesuit education, though they may never have had a Jesuit for a teacher or met a Jesuit in their four years of high school. Perhaps they encountered one for Masses or vocation promotion, or shaking hands with a Jesuit president at graduation, as even these numbers of leaders are declining.

As the parish convents and residences for teaching religious were vacated in the mass exodus from the schools and religious life itself following Vatican II, many were repurposed by the parishes. Many convents became parish offices and meeting rooms. Typically, a parish rectory had an office or two and perhaps a parlor to meet with parishioners.

Of course, in prior days before the escalation of parish staffs, the priests covered all the bases of sacramental preparation, visiting the sick, facility maintenance, managing the budget, visiting the school, etc. As clergy numbers declined, many lay men and women were prepared to assume leadership roles that were exclusively the domain of the priests and the sisters.

Among some of these new roles would be the Director of Music, Director of Liturgy, Director of Religious Education, Director of Youth Ministry, Director of Young Adult Ministry, Director of Programs for the Elderly, Director of the Catechumenate, Director of Sacrament Preparation for Marriage, Baptism, Penance, First Communion, etc., Director of Social Services (St. Vincent de Paul Society, food pantry, etc.), Director of Maintenance, Business Manager, the Parish Secretary, and possibly a Coordinator of the Directors.

Each of these would need a space to work, and a convent that was built for ten or twelve nuns proved an ideal setting for the legions of developing ministries and their needed office spaces. Parishes were becoming much more complex with the services which were being provided and needed. Consider and imagine the payroll and benefits for such operations.

While no one would be getting wealthy working for the church, there was still a desire to provide a just wage and good benefits to these employees. And while the teaching sisters were gone, a school still had its own budget to meet, of which approximately 80 percent goes to salaries and benefits. In a short period, parish finances went from management in an old cigar box filled with cash to QuickBooks, Excel, and greater professionalism and accountability.

While the sisters and other religious did not always leave these ministries overnight, the dramatic disappearance was staggering.[1] Many sisters did not like the direction that their communities were taking, especially leaving the ministry of education. A Presentation sister once commented that when many of the sisters of her community left parochial schools to work in foreign missions, they soon discovered what people wanted and needed most in these mission lands was education and schools; this was a bitter pill to swallow for some who sought what seemed to be more attractive ministries with the poor, but it was a reality.

Disadvantaged people with families are often in a catch-22 situation. This frustration of access to excellent schools was powerfully demonstrated in the 2010 documentary film *Waiting for Superman*. It is a sad development that at a time when urban areas are dotted with vacant Catholic school buildings and there are families eager for School Choice, there are few resources to answer the demand.

As Pope Francis commented during his pastoral visit to the United States in 2015, ". . . where would the Church in the United States be if it were not for the generous labors of women religious?" Indeed, a massive lacuna and financial strain formed that has been nearly impossible to fill as those religious who remained in their vows sought other ministries after massive departures.

True, these religious absorbed much of the costs of education with their monthly honorarium or stipend, but for better or worse, their generosity inflated a nearly unsustainable reality. Schools still struggle with the operational costs, with little or no buffer other than a subsidy from the parish or an endowment or rescue funds from the diocese. Unfortunately, most grade schools and high schools no longer have the presence of religious men and women. In those private schools, which are either owned by a community or sponsored by a community, with a board of trustees that governs the school and has fiduciary responsibilities, there is a growing phenomenon. Sadly, many of the secularizing programs that are assailing Catholic higher education are trickling down into private Catholic secondary and elementary schools, and to some degree into the diocesan schools. In the wake of 9/11 priests at one Catholic university were asked to wear their Roman collar instead of a mismatched tie and shirt and walk around campus to be visible and available to the community should someone want to talk with a religious type.

This is often repeated in schools when there is a suicide, an untimely death, or some other unanticipated catastrophe. However, given the dropping number of Catholics who attend Mass, and the disappearance of clergy from schools, why would a student seek out a priest if there is a minimal context for the relationship? It is not untypical for a priest to walk through a campus in his religious habit or black collar and get stares as if he just flew in from Tatooine or escaped from the labs at Area 51.

The assumption at work in asking for priests in these kinds of situations is well-intentioned but is premised on the affability and pastoral familiarity of Bing Crosby's Father O'Malley from *Going My Way* and *The Bells of St. Mary's*. Sudden crises cannot always microwave meaningful pastoral relationships.

One can describe this absentee landlord dynamic as a governance model. If a Catholic college/university or private secondary or elementary school is affiliated with a religious community such as the Franciscans or the Religious of the Sacred Heart, there is often an attempt to have the president and/or principal be a member of that order; however, those benches are getting thinner by the day.

It is also desirable to have a member of the said religious community to be the Director of Campus Ministry or the Vice President of Mission and Identity. These attempts to infuse the institution with some semblance of the order's charism and Catholicity are laudable attempts, but they are often too little, too late. Further, the board of directors can take another last-ditch effort to protect and promote the Catholicity of the institutions in another dimension of the governance rules.

Frequently, there will be a two-tiered board where a small group of about three or four members of the sponsoring religious community forming a tier [the Supervisory Board, often called the Board of Members] that has veto power over the larger board [Management Board]. So, for example, consider that a Management Board wanted to renovate the school's chapel.

Among the renovations, they hope to complement, or balance, the tabernacle which contains the Blessed Sacrament, with equally prominent and inclusive symbols from other religions and traditions such as a crescent and star, a statue of Vishnu, a statue of Pachamama, or a Totem Pole from a nearby tribe of the First Nation, etc.

One could hope that such a misguided consideration would not be pursued by the school's leadership, however if such a proposal moved forward and reached the board level, it might be because its costs exceed a certain amount of money, that would need board approval. Wishing to be *au courant* and politically correct, the board of members approve the project.

One could only expect and pray that the Supervisory Board of Members would awaken and veto the project and use the initiative to catechize about the prominence and importance of the Blessed Sacrament and why this is sacred to the mission of the institution.

Such a firewall would deter such insanity, but undoubtedly readers will be able to cite innumerable projects which directly undermine the Catholic mission of a school. Hence, the Supervisory Board of Members has a vital responsibility to keep the mission on track. In schools where there is just one tier, the task gets harder. Frequently, where the religious community has a presence on the board, the bylaws require a certain number of seats for the sponsoring religious community.

An example of such a formula would specify that one-quarter plus one of the total memberships of the board comprise members of the sponsoring religious community. The aim of this calculation is like the two-tiered board; should something profoundly compromising be promoted, the provincial could order the religious members to vote in such a way as to dash the proposal. However, as vocations to many of the mighty religious orders that reached their summit of impact in the 1960s have all but dried up, another tension has developed for the absentee landlords.

Many communities with so few active members are trying to hold on to institutions with a meaningful connection and usually that is through board membership. Unfortunately, serving on boards has become a full-time ministry for a few lucid members who can travel and take nourishment. Eventually, this will all play out to a vanishing point on the very near horizon as many of these orders shut off the lights. Trying to keep a toehold on these institutions in some meaningful way is elusive and without people in roles of leadership and serving on the teaching faculty, it is hard to imagine any substitute for the charism to survive.

Many orders have begun a sad and painful process of going out of existence. Their job is simply to care for the elderly members and make what accommodations are needed to transfer properties to another order or the diocese. There is a body of the Church's canon law which governs this transfer and liquidation of resources. Perhaps even more startling is the decision by many orders that they will no longer accept novices or candidates; this more than anything signals the end of the road.

If an order has a few applicants each year, there is some hope, but it will be diminished given the number of institutions it has and formation is a long road on which many do not persevere to final vows. Sadly, if an apostolic order coasts into just managing property and care for the elderly, the insular mission will probably not be attractive to many young people.

Perhaps to slow the decline, many orders of sisters have established a Lay Associate branch. Something akin to the Third Orders, men and women are welcome to affiliate in the spiritual and corporal works of the order. Today, many of the orders that had provided legions of teachers and administrators for the burgeoning Catholic schools from coast to coast now have new priorities.

Among some other new thrusts would be the Care for Creation, Environmental Issues, Racial Justice, Human Trafficking, Immigration Issues, Promotion of Non-violence, and establishing Economic Justice. There remain some orders of religious who are focused on schools, but most of the powerhouse orders of the last century have dwindled.

Yes, an elderly nun, brother, or priest of the community can show up on a Feast Day and give a talk, but the students are likely to forget what they heard. Orientation days can teach catch phrases, songs, history, and hagiographies related to the order or its mission. Who does not enjoy getting a new tee-shirt with some marketing information, or pens and mugs bearing a motto? There might be retreat days centered on a theme from the charism, but what does it really mean for the laity? Might these desperate efforts to stay relevant be self-delusional? Critical analysis of such situations may not be welcome.

The laity has their own spirituality and charism, and these form the emerging and dominant culture of the church. For the 2021–2022 school year, NCEA reported that the combined workforce of Catholic elementary and secondary schools was composed of 97.4% lay teachers, i.e., lay women (73.6%) and lay men (23.9%). So, in many ways, the diminishing role of religious begs the question. At any of these schools, there can be found a Dr., Mr., Ms., or Mrs. Chips who would have served for decades and multiple generations of a family.

Religious are usually assigned for four, six, or ten years and move to new assignments. Length of time does not dictate the impact of a person, but more time means more connections and more investment in the relationships. Clergy and religious infuse a school with a unique availability due to the nature of their vocations. Could Catholic schools be better off with no religious? Some leaders of some religious communities seem to think so, and in some schools where religious are present, some of the lay workers question their presence.

In meetings, which are composed of primarily lay folks who serve as board chairs and principals, provincials have been heard to gush about the glories of the contributions of the laity while ignoring the religious members of the community. Perhaps carried away with this theme and soaring rhetoric, some have said that the schools will be better run once the religious are out of the way.

The laity are much better educational leaders than priests and religious, and the schools can run effectively without the religious community. One Jesuit canon lawyer wryly responded to a superior's vision that lay colleagues would more competently carry the Society's institutions forward, that ". . . they are our lay colleagues until they find a better job or sue us!"

One priest who was present at such a meeting raised his hand and asked about the implications for the sacramental life of such a school with no clergy. "Since many families come to the school hoping that the school will offer Confession and Masses, who is supposed to provide these opportunities?" The provincial was tongue-tied at such an impertinent and unanticipated question and back-pedaled to say he did not mean that the sacraments were unimportant, and that priestly ministry was indeed important. Hmm . . .

It is not unheard of to pick up a sense of glee from community leaders talking about the *gift of diminishment*. Some orders are opening sponsored grammar schools in very poor areas where the needs are great; however, there will not be boots on the ground in those schools from the community, but the absentee landlords will try to inspire things and prop up the vision of the founders with some minimal formation.

While members of the religious community will not likely be missioned to such a school due to dwindling numbers, the affiliation and bylaws will have some protocols which require board members from said community, but the day-to-day connection with the community will be negligible. Try this exercise: Check out a Catholic high school sponsored or owned by a religious order and see if the board members are listed on the website.

Compare the number of board members of religious to those religious members who are full-time in the school. Odds are that there are more board members than worker bees in the school. Of course, the new project will completely depend on the brand name of the religious community and the benefactors of that community. If the order sponsors other works in that city, the order will be spread thin with little presence, if any, in those institutions.

The average person will support 4.5 charities, so imagine what kinds of causes a Catholic might champion. Leroy supports his high school, his college, his parish, and the local zoo. Maria supports her parish, the archdiocese, a pro-life office, and her college alma mater. People will split their educational dollars, much like folks do with the ubiquitous second collections at Sunday Mass. If a person is planning to put $20.00 in the collection basket this week, but there is a second collection, each may likely get $10.00.

This is especially true of the multiple schools operated by a particular order; some donors will sometimes manufacture a reason not to give to one in favor of another. Leadership of religious communities do not seem to consider the impact such new schools will have upon existing missions. There is a great deal of presumption of goodwill and sometimes naivete.

Fortunately, there are some orders that are growing and are committed to Catholic schools. The Dominican Sisters of Mary Mother of the Eucharist are attracting many vocations and have legions of requests for their sisters from bishops and pastors (Mother Assumpta Long, OP, has stated that the number of requests from bishops and pastors for teaching sisters is north of four hundred annually).

The Nashville Dominican Sisters of Saint Cecelia, the Carmelite Sisters of Alhambra, the Franciscan Sisters of the Martyr Saint George, the Apostles of the Sacred Heart of Jesus, the Dominican Friars of the St. Joseph Province, and the Society of Jesus are among the orders that have invested mightily in education and see a regular pipeline of new vocations, though for some of these, the numbers are not robust.

There are other communities, and those schools will be blessed with the presence of religious men and women who are actually present in the schools. Building rapport and relationships are key in the development of young people and to nurture collegiality among adults.

However, for anyone who has a nostalgic sensibility for Catholic schools as they were up to the 1960s full of sisters, religious brothers, and priests, there is no turning back the clock. Cardinal Dolan of New York has informally described the *Used to Be Church*. As he was being introduced to the Archdiocese of New York, people would point out such things as:

- There used to be an orphanage here established by Mother Seton that the Sisters of Charity ran;
- Over there used to be a parish high school that was staffed by the Irish Christian Brothers;
- That closed parish used to have the largest Catholic grade school here with over 1,500 students;
- Where that shopping center is, used to be a massive motherhouse;
- See that nightclub, there used to be a parish here with Masses almost every hour and each Mass was packed;
- There used to be a high school seminary here that was staffed by the Vincentians;
- There used to be a Benedictine Convent of Perpetual Adoration there.

Every diocese and bishop could easily take such a wistful tour down Memory Lane, but those days are only found in the diocesan archives.

If Vatican II emphasized the role of the laity, the time has certainly arrived when faithful men and women will take roles of leadership in Catholic schools. If truth be told, they have been doing so for decades. Lay colleagues have been a part of Catholic schools from the beginning. Since most of the membership of the Church is composed of lay men and women, it makes sense that these disciples are well poised to share their faith and to model a firm commitment to the spiritual project.

Catholic elementary schools have been leaders in this trend, away from the charism and presence of a religious order. When the particular order was at the school, it made sense that the school culture would be infused with the traditions and legacy of the Sisters of Mercy and Mother Catherine McAuley.

However, soon after the sisters had departed, what does it really mean to cultivate those unique spiritual principles of the charism? Not that these elements are opposed to anything in being a faithful Catholic, but it seems to shine the spotlight on an empty cobwebbed corner or historical footnote, or the *School that Used to Be*. What might that spiritual project be for the laity?

Good catechesis would be at the core of the spiritual formation of the laity, both for the school leaders and students. This intellectual approach should not be considered a task that is completed with twelfth grade, but an ongoing lifelong strategy. Faithful attendance at weekly Mass and regular celebration of the Sacrament of Confession would be at the heart of one's prayer life.

Going hand in hand with the regular celebration of the sacraments would be to cultivate a personal prayer life with devotion to the Blessed Virgin Mary and the saints. Faith should not be relegated to tagging a spiritual base on Sundays. Service projects are a popular means of living the faith and show up in the Final Exam described in Matthew 25:31–46.

Clearly, supporting the Church and its missions is another example. Students are introduced to philanthropy in Catholic schools. While adopting pagan babies was once a well-intentioned activity in the Holy Childhood Association, it taught a valuable lesson about evangelization and caring for people around the world. These were the lessons that the religious men and women promoted, and they remain important elements of a Catholic school and the laity has proven to be excellent stewards of these essential elements of the Catholic school.

These elements that should inspire young people are all done in a community of believers. The parish, the elementary school, and the high school all form important circles of relationships that center on the teachings of Jesus and His Church. Parents begin the teaching with their children at home and the school builds on these lessons, deepening the spiritual lives of students. These are not works that one needs to be a member of a religious community to lead.

Of the remaining religious communities who affiliate with schools, many of their members do not want to be lone rangers in operating a school. A young religious was sent to a high school as the only member of his community to learn how to teach. Besides his teaching duties, he was made the Director of Mission. Sadly, he was sent to be mentored, but was entrusted with serious leadership responsibilities for which he was not prepared.

This kind of lone ranger mentality or filling a slot is not untypical with the diminishing numbers of active religious, coupled with a community's aversion to the educational apostolate and attraction to boutique ministries. This kind of grasp on a school will not be generating much interest in vocations.

One element that prompts young people to consider a religious vocation is the possibility to work in an apostolate where members of a community are working together and enjoying one another's company. Hence, the few young people who are open to considering a vocation are gravitating towards the orders with a clear identity and mission and not to those who are living separately in apartments with minimal community life or contact.

Students appreciate and enjoy seeing the religious family and how they interact with one another. Do they pray together? How do they dress? What do they do? What are their values? Do they enjoy one another's company? Do they genuinely care about one another? Are they seen together at school functions? The schools that have a constellation of religious have better odds of attracting students to consider a religious vocation, but for many orders, the traditional pipeline of promoting vocations has been irrevocably broken.

Many may wonder or hope that there might be a Spiritual Awakening in the near future. With a Church that has been so wounded and under constant criticism from a predictably hostile media coupled with the deep decline of believers attending Mass, it is difficult to imagine this aircraft carrier being turned around soon. The next twenty-five to fifty years will see many religious communities shut off their lights.

Fortunately, there will be some orders that will thrive and continue to attract new recruits. One provincial of an order of sisters who primarily work in education commented: "We love Christ and His Church and are here to do the work of promoting the faith. If God wants us to continue this work, He needs to get on the ball and send us the recruits. We're doing everything we can." There is a great sense of freedom and wisdom in such an assessment of the current situation.

Priests, sisters, and brothers working in schools will be rarer and a more nostalgic walk down in history. However, one of the growing considerations for these communities will be how to let go or turn over the work to the laity. It is becoming increasingly difficult to even maintain a meaningful presence in those schools where there is still an institutional affiliation.

Some wonder if an order would be better off investing what few members they have in just a few apostolates, or would the current situation of spreading the few members among multiple works be the ticket? It is a good and fair question. Provincials need to consider the relationships that have been built with alumni and how committed those folks will be in supporting a project that is abandoned by the order.

In admissions work, it is not an unusual question to be asked: "How many sisters, priests, or brothers work here?" This question carries a hope that there might be at least a few standard bearers of the order to interact with their children. Frankly, teachers will have the greatest impact on students. Yes, Principals, Presidents, Directors of Mission, and Directors of Campus Ministry, or Chairs of the Religion Department all contribute valuable leadership skills.

However, it is the day-to-day interactions that teachers have with students where the most powerful impact is made. The disposition of many orders in wanting to navigate the ship with key leadership roles is noble, but if there are no other boots on the ground from the order to support those leaders, it is inching towards the absentee landlord phenomena.

Many religious communities are not encouraging their junior members to be prepared for these leadership roles. In the past, members of a community were basically told what their mission would be and given opportunities for the training and necessary preparation to fulfill it. Stories are told where there were colossal mismatches of someone with an English degree being handed a chemistry textbook and to stay a week ahead of the students, but after Vatican

II, initial efforts were made to assign a better match between institutional needs and the skills and interests of the vowed member.

It was not unusual for someone to be tapped to be a principal or school leader with little or no administrative experience, but there was plenty of opportunity for mentoring and on-the-job training. Summers frequently saw university administration programs housed in their Schools of Education swell with those new leaders as they tried to get the professional credential or degree needed to carry out their duties.

The days leading up to the great exodus of religious in the 1960s also saw many sisters who had gone directly from the novitiate to the classroom with only a high school diploma and a few years of spiritual formation in the order, spending their summers gaining an undergraduate degree and teaching credential. While things have changed for many orders that exited the schools, orders like the Dominican Sisters of Mary Mother of the Eucharist send their sisters to work with degrees and teaching credentials in hand.

Among the high schools and grade schools that are currently led by a religious sister, priest, or brother, these institutions will face the following question when that leader steps down as principal or president with an expectation that this is a slot that the order has a responsibility to fill: "Are there any (Franciscans, Servites, or Sisters of Charity) out there that we can tap?" The order's answer is increasingly a disconcerting "no."

When school boards face this transition of a priest or religious stepping aside, they naturally think of the religious community that has historically held such positions. The vocation crisis has been sufficiently covered in the press, but perhaps people think their school's situation is unique and will have a place of privilege with the sponsoring community. Such schools are finding that a major transition is about to take place that will probably not be reversed.

The Church in the United States is witnessing tremendous changes and many of these are changes in terms of diminishment which will present challenges. Flourishing Catholic schools had always been one of the most promising aspects of the Church's history and legacy, with the legions of dedicated sisters, brothers, and priests providing the backbone and workforce of these institutions.

Suddenly, much of that workforce was removed and those religious orders had to think about how they intended to move forward in their relationship with schools where they supplied teachers and administrators, or that they owned and/or sponsored.

During the 1960s many of the private schools that were owned and governed by a religious community transitioned to separate incorporation where a board of trustees would technically own the school and the religious community would be the sponsoring entity. This freed communities and provinces from endless litigious entanglements and financial disasters.

As noted earlier, some schools maintained a two-level board with some retention over policy and direction should critical Catholic issues get compromised. Now, decades later, these same orders may look back on those steps of relinquishing ownership to the boards as a first step of exiting the project.

In many ways, the move to separate incorporation was a prudent decision, but probably not an easy one at the time. Most of those orders who established those schools would have had to purchase the land, get it zoned, raise money not only for the land but money to construct the facility. These efforts all took place with a largely immigrant church, and their discretionary funds were scarce. The various orders were also building and establishing motherhouses and houses of formation, all of which cost a great deal.

Hence the investment in establishing schools was considerable and came with untold sacrifices by the community and those who would use the schools. Carnivals, raffles, Bingo, Friday fish frys, all tried to raise the money. So, for the orders to sign over the schools could not have been easy for anyone, but again, it was a wise and farsighted decision.

The separate incorporation decision may have been a forward pass thrown and caught, symbolizing the ultimate withdrawal or exit from the schools. The next step was maintaining a presence by covering some of the leadership bases that were described above, such as Director of Campus Ministry, Principal, or President.

Following this development was the phenomenon of the absentee landlord having religious on the board. Some of these religious have become professional board members by serving in this role as a full-time mission. As this group ages and becomes incapacitated, what then? The bylaws will be changed to reflect their disappearance.

While many orders have established those lay affiliations, those men and women do not have any canonical standing, nor would they have any legal standing, so it is doubtful that they could represent the religious community. Besides, they are lay men and women who have their own expertise and wisdom to offer. At some point, some of these schools will transition to full lay leadership and staffing. That scenario is already unfolding in many schools as the sponsoring religious order diminishes and those few members can no longer keep up with the demands of serving on boards.

All of this suggests that dramatic changes are underway. Would it be better and farsighted to make plans to implement these transitions now or wait until the pool is completely dried up? Can schools move from a place of strength by changing their bylaws and expressing gratitude to the sponsoring community? Communities could still visit and be welcomed as honored guests whose community ancestors bequeathed a monumental project to them they can no longer sustain. Students at such schools should know their history and how they are a part of something much bigger.

This chapter calls to mind the pioneering work of Elisabeth Kubler-Ross and her description of the process of grieving over a death. Though intended to describe the experience of human beings dying, there is much wisdom for organizations and institutions. Those stages are denial, anger, bargaining, depression, and acceptance. One must wonder where different communities are on this spectrum.

The process offers tremendous implications for the dispositions and decisions that govern the communities about their own existence and the works that have slipped away from them. The stages can be instructive for framing how to understand various decisions of religious communities and how they face what will be, for some, an inevitable transition.

Some groups will be in denial, thinking that a bumper crop of novices is just around the corner. Some are angry at the institutional church for all kinds of reasons. The current approach with the absentee landlord model seems to echo the stage of bargaining as communities try to hold on to their roles by the thinnest of threads. Along with the bargaining and attempts to be relevant without being present, one might think that depression runs through all this diminishment.

How could these communities not lament the days when the schools were animated by the presence, charism, and vitality of their orders? Many grade schools from coast to coast have heard the sisters say farewell. These women were the pillar of the leadership and teaching posts at countless grade schools.

Often enough, their departure was a first slippery step for a school that was on the skids. After their departure, some schools moved forward in strength and stayed the course. Other schools boarded up the project. This was not a result of the sisters leaving, but more a case of many factors: fewer students, families moving away, a deteriorating neighborhood, etc. But there is a lesson when looking at the current number of Catholic schools that are thriving and operating.

These successful schools that do not have religious working in them show the strength of the laity and their vocations to lead these schools. As the future of Catholic schools unfolds, the role of religious men and women will continue to diminish to a large extent. In ten to twenty-five years there will be greater losses to religious communities and their sponsored projects. Those schools that are fortunate to have religious in them will harvest a special blessing with the presence of the entire Church membership present. Schools are not alone in these developments, healthcare and social services that were the domain of religious communities have been on the same downward trajectory of diminishment.

KEY IDEAS IN CHAPTER 4

- Diminishment of the Teaching Orders of Sisters, Brothers, and Priests
- Contributed Services of Religious Women and Men Camouflaged the Actual Costs
- Schools Sponsored by Religious Try to Maintain Some Leadership through Boards
- Absentee Landlord Phenomenon
- Orders of Religious Establish Associate Branches to Boost Numbers
- Religious Leaders Cheering as Reins of Leadership Are Passed to the Laity
- Implications for Fundraising with Fewer Religious
- Vocation Prospects
- Teachers Have Greater Impact on Relationships with Students and Alumni
- Separate Incorporation for Private Schools

NOTES

1. Caruso, 2012

Chapter 5

Athletics

The Gift that Keeps Scoring!

Probably three-quarters of students in Catholic elementary and secondary schools take part in sports. The field, the swimming pool, the bowling alley, and the gym are other classrooms where important lifelong lessons are learned. Athletics provides students with opportunities to condition, to work together for a common goal, to learn how to take joy in the success of others, to absorb failure, and to have a good deal of fun. Donald Kitson is credited with a valuable insight: *"The true measure of a man is his dignity in defeat and humility in victory."*

Along with the psychological benefits of athletics, young people are developing into adults. The ancient Greeks spoke of the importance of a fit mind and fit body, and everything we know from modern medicine and healthy aging has confirmed these insights from antiquity. Exercise is a valuable and necessary endeavor and outlet for young men and women.

In every school, Physical Education is a class that everyone takes, often with an admonition to explore an activity that a person enjoys and can be a lifelong physical activity. One does not have to be a marathon runner. Biking, walking, team sports for adults are on the radar screens of coaches and Physical Education teachers. Like any teacher in every discipline, there is a hope that there is a spark of appreciation and perhaps a lifelong interest in the students. It is also an important venue to burn off energy.

Athletics are a necessary ingredient to any Catholic school. In fact, a successful athletic program can only help the stability of the school as it draws in so many constituents. More people will show up for a Friday night football game than for a concert or play. Basketball also draws crowds and generates lots of positive energy. Athletics seem to be part of the American DNA and in a school, a great program can generate lots of support, enthusiasm, and positive public relations. Oftentimes, the press carries sporting news and this shapes a perception of a school in the wider community.

Of course, these published stories can go many directions. In addition to the triumphs and district achievements, poor sportsmanship can also catch the eye of a reporter. A good athletic program is worth the time and energy of an administration. A well-run program will benefit the individual athletes as well as strengthen a school as a pillar of the neighborhood and school community. Alumni especially keep an eye on their alma mater's athletic program.

For those who wish to pursue a particular sport, there is usually a generous menu of possibilities. Jesuit Father Patrick Kelly, SJ, has researched athletics and written extensively on their history in the schools and their importance. He has especially highlighted the connection between spirituality and athletics.[1] So, there should be a great deal to celebrate regarding the world of athletics and indeed there is. A powerful example is the liturgical season of Lent.

Lent is a time when the entire Church is called upon to go into Spiritual Spring Training in anticipation of the great mysteries of Holy Week and celebration of the central Christian Feast of Easter. It includes fasting, time in prayer, and almsgiving. These traditional practices are to strengthen the spiritual muscles and make practitioners more limber and attentive as disciples. These spiritual exercises also target some of the inner flabbiness that has accumulated.

One can easily see how the entire cycle of a sport is analogous to the spiritual life. Recognition that you need to get into better shape; taking steps to train and get in better shape; humbly listening to expertise and advice; making choices that are disciplined and focused on a goal; working as part of a team while doing your best are all valuable elements in the world of sports and the spirit.

Both elementary and secondary schools rally around various sports. Football and basketball particularly draw large crowds on a Friday night. Parents, grandparents, students, some faculty members, and fans near and far enjoy turning out to support a team. Especially in those climates which limit outdoor activity during the winter months, high school basketball provides a delightful evening of fellowship and an opportunity to show school spirit and build the community.

For many grade schools, their schedules might be played primarily on Fridays and Saturdays. Parents can be seen watching Kindergarten Soccer teams, no doubt realizing how they will be spending Saturday mornings for the next several years hauling children to games and being enthusiastic fans. Like many endeavors, delivering a sports program is not thorn free.

In high schools, running a close second to the principal as the recipient of unsought headaches, is the Athletic Director [AD]; he or she has one of the most challenging jobs in the school; it can also bring a good deal of personal satisfaction in seeing the growth and development of young people, which must be one of the attractors to the position.

At the college level, people are often amazed to see the salaries that are paid to Athletic Directors; one should not be too surprised as these school leaders earn it. There are endless problems associated with delivering a good program or any program. In the high schools there might be an assistant athletic director who helps with innumerable tasks. Consider the school's athletic calendar.

Once the school calendar has been set, the Athletic Department must look at scheduling practices and competitions for Fall, Winter, and Spring sports. Most Catholic schools are under tremendous pressure to find the appropriate spaces for multiple sports and practices and generally will need to utilize public parks and/or rent facilities. Fields are particularly in high demand; there is rarely enough real estate at a school to accommodate every sport. Once these practices and games are set, transportation becomes an issue. Arranging for busses to transport the teams becomes quite an endeavor.

Some schools own their own busses or vans which coaches may drive once they have received the proper licensing and approval. The school will have protocols about the use of these vehicles especially about the care for such, which is often ignored by the teams and drivers. Complaints form a steady stream to the Athletic Director: the vehicle has little or no fuel; traffic conditions are horrible; there is no time for a stop at the gas station; students left garbage and trash in the van; the bus was not parked in its proper spot and cannot be found; the van was broken but the last user did not report the situation; the vehicle smells like the Stink House at the zoo, etc.

Naturally, these common courtesies are discovered by the next coach driving the vehicle, and often, at a moment when things are running behind, and time is of the essence; not unlike the use of shared cars in a religious community that shares a fleet of dilapidated used cars from Cuba. So, begins, the endless reminders to all parties that fill faculty email boxes about courtesy and use of these vans and busses.

In the world of sports, at all levels, there are major safety and legal concerns that demand attention. Clay Burnett of Final Forms, a company that offers various resources and support for the management of athletic programs, noted the following key issues that leaders of athletic programs need to have considered and have plans in place to address: 1. Liabilities for Injuries, 2. Concussion Management, 3. Social Media Issues, 4. Hazing, 5. Sexual Harassment, 6. Transgender Athlete Policies, 7. Disabilities, 8. Title IX, 9. Emergency Contacts, Procedures, and Protocols, and 10. Having Proper Documentation to Satisfy District, State, and Federal Regulations.[2]

Liabilities for Injuries: At various times during the school year, the halls and school corridors might look like a MASH Unit with all the student injuries from athletics. Broken limbs, torn muscles, casts, crutches, boots, slings, all keep the medical world sufficiently busy and orthopedic physicians from being on the welfare rolls. While students need to have evidence of medical insurance coverage to take part in athletics, a school can still be in a vulnerable position and exposed to litigation.

This often gets pursued under the aegis of negligence, i.e., a "... failure to behave with the level of care that someone of ordinary prudence would have exercised under the same circumstances."

Imagine a coach allowing an underage student to drive the school's van to a game and there is an accident with injuries; the school will have major legal problems. Another situation might be from an adult allowing athletes to have a victory beer. Equally problematic examples would be a practice during a raging thunderstorm or during a heat advisory (synthetic turf can be 40–70 degrees warmer than the outside temperature on a sunny day). Faulty equipment and ignoring horseplay are also typical scenarios.

Concussions: Burnett noted: "In recent years, concussions have taken center stage in the world of athletics, largely due to studies finding connections between playing football and CTE injury that occurs after repeated head trauma." Like all schools, the Catholic world has been attentive to this growing concern. At times, the media has fanned the flames of worry over youth-related athletics, particularly with football, but soccer and other field sports are not without concern. Some even wondered with all the hype if schools might drop football because of the concussion risks.

All fifty states have laws governing concussion issues in schools with Washington State to be the first to have such a law. All other states baked into their legislation most of the following points: Coach education, removing athletes suspected of head injuries, return to practice, protocols, or play only after being cleared by a medical professional, return to play clearance, and parents signing forms about the concussion awareness and issues.

Social Media Issues: Burnett cited a Pew Study stating 95 percent of teenagers have a smartphone and a large part of the day is spent on the phone using various programs. As noted in the chapter on technology many are the problems this poses. The *New York Post*'s gossip page has a subtitle warning: "IF YOU DON'T WANT IT ON PAGE SIX, DON'T DO IT." This would be a good mantra for athletes and coaches as ubiquitous cameras are constantly rolling and sharing bad behavior is only a click away.

Hazing: When a student is hazed, the values of a Catholic school are being transgressed. No Catholic school tolerates hazing and if it is discovered, it should be promptly remedied. Students who participate in athletics are trying to be part of a group and find a way to fit in. Hazing isolates a person while being humiliated and tormented. No doubt, the perpetrators would say they were just teasing and meant nothing by the incident. Hazing leaves deep wounds and victims do not forget. Sadly, hazing can lead to other risky behaviors that are dangerous or even deadly.

A team party might include consuming alcohol or drugs in a large quantity to the amusement of the team veterans. Students might be asked to do some feat of physical prowess that involves something dangerous; ". . . you have to jump out of a second story window onto the trampoline below, everyone does it." Proper and appropriate supervision in the locker room is essential as much mischief can be concocted and executed here; much like a lunch period, students need to take care of business and move along; unstructured time is not always a good commodity for young people.

Sexual Harassment: Since the beginning of this millennium Catholic institutions have been hypersensitive and alert to matters relating to interpersonal boundaries between every imaginable configuration. Coaches and teachers are regularly attending professional development seminars relating to Sexual Harassment in the workplace and clearly these guidelines apply between adults and most especially between adults and young people. Students are taught about respect and proper relations, but learning, knowing, and doing are all different realities.

The RAINN Institute (Rape, Abuse & Incest National Network) offers various resources for anti–sexual violence. They state:

> Sexual harassment includes unwelcome sexual advances, requests for sexual favors, and other verbal or physical harassment of a sexual nature in the workplace or learning environment, according to the Equal Employment Opportunity Commission. Sexual harassment does not always have to be specifically about sexual behavior or directed at a specific person. For example, negative comments about women as a group may be a form of sexual harassment. Although sexual harassment laws do not usually cover teasing or offhand comments, these behaviors can also be upsetting and have a negative emotional effect. (RAINN n.d.)

Because athletics often enough place people in intimate physical proximity with one another while competing, it may give people a false sense of security in that they feel they can say and do things that are under the radar. Mean Girl behavior or raunchy locker room banter can trip the wires of inappropriate conduct and cross lines. Therefore, adult behavior, appropriate supervision, and role modeling are critically important, and for coaches to correct any such infractions. This is precisely an area where the teachings of the Church provide a powerful blueprint for healthy relationships and interactions.

Transgender Athlete Policies: Pope Francis has reiterated the consistent teachings on this topic in his encyclical *Amoris Laetitia* when he stated:

> The young need to be helped to accept their own body as it was created, for thinking that we enjoy absolute power over our own bodies turns, often subtly, into thinking that we enjoy absolute power over creation. An appreciation of

our body as male or female is also necessary for our own self-awareness in an encounter with others different from ourselves. In this way we can joyfully accept the specific gifts of another man or woman, the work of God the Creator, and find mutual enrichment.

One can see the maelstrom especially in the world of women's athletics of men transitioning to female and mopping up all the awards and records. Catholic schools have no compelling reason to head down this path, but then again, who knows where this culture battle will lead?

Some biological females who falsified baptismal records were admitted to seminaries and this has sent Church leaders into a tailspin over application protocols (Schneible 2022). In January 2022 the Archdiocese of Milwaukee promulgated a useful document (Catechesis and Policy on Questions Concerning Gender Theory 2022). It offers a balanced pastoral response to the entire question and will be of use to many schools and athletic programs when the question presents itself.

Title IX: This legislation states that schools must offer equal opportunities for girls and boys and institutions cannot discriminate based on gender. Hence, if a school has a soccer program for boys, it must offer one for girls. If there is not a girl's football team, the school must welcome girls to try out for the football team. However, this legislation only applies in government/public schools. Religious elementary and secondary schools are exempt from Title IX and have great leeway in their interpretation of it. Just the same, the positive spirit and benefits of Title IX are found in Catholic schools. Schools see the tremendous benefits of offering an expansive menu of athletic opportunities for both boys and girls to the degree the operational budget and staffing can support the activities.

Emergency Contacts, Procedures, and Protocols: Catholic schools have such information available and on hand; these represent good administration and care for students as well as adults. When emergency situations occur, getting the right information in a timely manner is not always easy. Consider calling an ambulance for an unconscious player. First and foremost is the safety and well-being of the student so multiple actions need to be done at the same time. Getting the student the help they need and simultaneously informing the parents if they are not at the event.

Students who are diabetic or have other special health issues need to have these disclosed so that appropriate attention can be given. Diocesan policies help all schools to make sure that their procedures are in good order. Over the years as the complexities of good care have increased, schools have kept pace through the guidance of medical and legal experts. Families can be confident that their sons and daughters are being well cared for and if not, the school should be open to any suggestions to improve these protocols.

Having Proper Documentation to Satisfy District, State, and Federal Regulations: Athletics is governed by many bodies. Most dioceses have a Catholic League which structures the athletics in the schools and defines many of the activities, but schools are not always limited to the governance of this league. There would be a wide variety of protocols mainly determined by geography and where a school is located. A Catholic school in a small rural area will not have many other Catholic schools to play in sports, hence they will compete with local government schools.

Conversely, a Catholic school located in a large archdiocese will have many opportunities within the Catholic school system, but even there, they may not be confined to these. States designate leagues and distinctions based on the number of students in a school for competition. In a large city, the all-boys Christian Brothers School of 1,400 students will probably not be competing with a coed diocesan high school of 300 students; the odds would not be favorable for obvious reasons. A final important consideration is that of financing athletics.

Each sport comes with a different price tag and some programs are extremely expensive while others are modest. Some costs are subsidized by the students who participate but then there are the fixed costs that are often not considered. Salaries for coaches, trainers, and other health professionals. Outfitting volleyball, football, or lacrosse teams differs greatly from that of the basketball team or soccer. Some of the more expensive sports such as crew and hockey are usually club sports, meaning they are based in the community with a loosely coupled affiliation with the school.

Sometimes problems arise with the administration of these club sports since they are not under the direct jurisdiction of a school. Generally, there are good relations between the club sport and the school as the sport is representing the school and in the minds of everyone there is no distinction. Schools will want to keep in good conversation about the hiring of coaches and their formation to represent the school.

In the high school world, many coaches are not full-time employees at the school, which can be problematic; this is likely true of Catholic elementary schools, but more on that later. The ideal situation is to have a full-time teacher or administrator who is also the head coach for a particular sport. While all teachers are expected to sponsor and moderate a club, this is typically done without compensation; these duties are baked into one's salary. However, coaching earns an additional stipend because of the time commitment and investment of the coach.

The French teacher who is also the Girls' Softball coach, or Science teacher who is the Boys' Head Basketball coach, are increasingly and unfortunately, rare to find. Teachers and staff who facilitate athletics bring a great deal of expertise and street credit to all they do. Foremost, hopefully, they have been socialized into the school's mission. They always understand the importance of behavior and school decorum. There is not a dichotomy between the classroom and the sport.

Unfortunately, schools often rely on hiring a part-time coach for a particular sport. These coaches can be excellent assets to the school's mission, but they can also be the source of much trouble. When such coaches are hired, it is only on their expertise and experience to deliver a safe and good program. Background checks are conducted to make certain the person is free and clear of any criminal activity, etc. Sadly, and most often, schools provide little in the way of an orientation to the mission of the school.

The coach is interviewed and if he or she meets the criteria, he or she is given a coaching handbook with the school's expectations and the necessary information to get the program up and running. Farsighted schools have developed ongoing orientation programs that highlight the value of integrating spirituality into their sports programs; *nemo dat quod non habet.* What might such a program hope to achieve?

First, it would affirm that their role and contribution is valued beyond their sport and they play an important role in the school community. Such a session might reflect parts of a general faculty orientation given at the beginning of the year and repeated for Winter and Spring sports seasons. There would be time for the school's leadership team to talk about the importance of athletics and the expectations of coaches. Ideally, these part-time coaches would be practicing Catholics, but that is an idealistic expectation.

Coaches need to know about school decorum, and that use of foul language and bullying are not tolerated. Expected behavior while playing a sport and in the locker room need to be identified and these things can never be emphasized too often. It is not unusual to walk past a practice field and to hear some of the foulest language imaginable coming from coaches. You will sometimes hear a defense such as: *"C'mon! Boys will be boys! Those kids hear and say worse."* This is a most unfortunate dynamic and needs to be faced head on when discovered. But after a thorough orientation about expectations, infractions need to be documented.

Given the access that most people have to the internet, there is no shortage of reporting; reporting that can be factual or fictitious driven by the digital rumor mill. Coaches need to know that students and others are always watching and very little is done privately, and student athletes are learning about what is important. So, if a coach throws a temper tantrum in the locker room after an upsetting loss and is cursing and verbally abusing players, it will most surely get back to the Athletic Director and/or principal through parents and sometimes the students.

School leadership will need to follow up with these incidents, which unfortunately, are not rare. It is hard to imagine a season or year where there is not some kerfuffle along these lines. These formation/orientation sessions can also allow the coaches to ask questions and get clarification. Though many do not enjoy attending such meetings and sit like sullen children kept after school for detention, they are essential to running a good athletic program that is mission driven.

Some coaches can get inflated egos and it is not unheard of to see narcissists in these roles. Their athletes adore them, and they have great cachet in the coaching world. However, sometimes these folks can cross a line. One such coach was disciplining students by having them do something embarrassing. Students arriving late to practice were told to practice without an essential part of their uniform. Some students and parents did not think it was a big deal; however, some students were mortified and afraid to confront the popular part-time coach. The coach's directive undermined everything the school held about the dignity of the students and culture of respect that the school tried to cultivate.

Some excellent administrative advice was offered in the form of a question by a retired police sergeant that cuts through layers of malarkey: "*ABC 7 News is on the front porch of the school with cameras rolling; what do you want to defend?*" That question is worth at least three graduate hours in school administration and/or communications.

When things get out of hand with adolescents and a line is crossed by them or the coach, that question shines a floodlight on the right path to follow and helps avoid sweeping things under the rug or dismissing a situation as not being a big deal. Athletics is governed by rules and protocols and there are many Sergeants at Arms prepared to alert the world to infractions; enter the world of disgruntled parents.

Parents make huge sacrifices for the children to be in a Catholic school and this is beyond paying tuition. Participation in a sport usually incurs additional costs for a program fee, uniforms, etc. Many of these parents also played sports in their day and they genuinely know a sport and will offer advice on how to improve a program. Parents are also called upon to host gatherings and meals for a team and they will undoubtedly form very close friendships with the other families who are on the same team as their son or daughter.

On Senior Nights, families will go to great lengths to show support and appreciation for the graduating team members. Gyms and fields are decorated with large posters honoring the seniors. Balloon arches in the school's colors are constructed to create a festive atmosphere. At the end of a season, there is usually a festive banquet when accolades and awards are given.

Most of these initiatives are funded through the generous support of the parents that go above and beyond any fees for playing. These are wonderful initiatives and go a long way in building up the particular sport and supporting the entire school community. However, the old administrative observation that you spend 90 percent of your time with 10 percent of the people can sometimes be apropos of parents with students playing sports.

After tryouts for a particular sport a coach may have to make cuts. Why does a coach think it is necessary to make cuts, because some sports do not have cuts? This poses a good question, but a convincing case can be made for the cuts, unless it is your son or daughter who gets cut.

Given the amount of practice time that a student must invest in a sport, a coach knows what talent he or she is seeking for a successful season; this coach can also spot aspirants who will never play unless there are a few moments left on the clock and the home team is winning by a large margin. Coaches do not want to be babysitters for such students who tend to get distracted and frustrated from lack of engagement and this becomes problematic for team spirit and pulling together.

However, some sports can accommodate a "no cut" policy; within those worlds students seem to understand how things work and are fine with the opportunity to practice and be part of something larger. When a student gets cut, a coach can expect a certain amount of howling. This grievance may even rise to the Athletic Director and Principal. This can also lead to a great deal of pot-stirring and bellyaching to everyone and anyone who will listen. It is a difficult situation.

One of the many dimensions and tasks of growing up, is finding an activity at school that one enjoys. Not everyone will be a math whiz and be invited to related competitions. Some people are not comfortable standing on a stage singing or acting. Not everyone is suited to be a Cross Country runner. But there is time during grade school and high school to find those extracurricular areas that are enjoyable and that accentuate a student's talents. Most parents understand how this works, but in the world of athletics, there is often a steady pipeline of complaints. Cuts represent one predictable flash point each season, another is informally evaluating the coach and the program.

Anyone who has a public role is going to be praised and/or criticized for what they say and do. Coaches are important role models for young people so finding good coaches is worth all the time and energy to make sure they are practicing Catholics and/or understand the importance of the school's mission. Unfortunately, they can become easy targets of complaints.

Often enough, no matter how general the complaint—"*She runs a lousy basketball program; where'd they find her?*"—what is hidden behind the general complaint is a particular and unspoken grumble that runs something like "*Why is my daughter not getting more court time? She would save this pathetic program.*" Even though other parents might disagree, for the sake of peace they nod in agreement. This then can be insidious and build into a movement through the internet and chat rooms. If something like this gets out of control, a parent will have to be confronted by the Athletic Director or Principal.

Though this is rare, occasionally an adult will appear inebriated and become a major problem at an event. With booze having washed away all filters of discretion, an adult can scream and curse the referees, the coach, opponents, or whoever is in earshot, creating a major embarrassment for the school as well as the associated family, and most certainly someone's son or daughter. It is a very unpleasant task to ask such a person to leave the event and follow up with an awkward conversation. Athletic Directors are on constant alert to help keep events in good order.

Student evaluations of coaches are absolutely essential. It would be good to ask students for feedback midway through a season and at the end. If evaluations are only summative and gathered at the end of a season, some important problem may have gone unaddressed as well as some constructive feedback left on the table. Just like evaluations in the classroom when assessments are left to the end of a course or semester, that teacher or coach cannot adjust something for that particular group.

Yes, the feedback can be useful for future classes or teams, but that adjustment may not have been an issue for another class. In short, having a few feedback opportunities can only strengthen a program. In athletics, students typically wish to perform their best for coaches. The relationship between a student athlete and coach is a powerful bond and one that students will often carry forward for a lifetime.

Alumni events are filled with people recalling wonderful memories of their time playing sports. Lifetime friendships are forged and there is untold good will that comes from the athletic program. It is an area of the school that garners widespread attention and support. In fact, after financial aid, it could be one of the most popular areas of a school in which to raise money. Alumni usually are eager to support facility improvements or projects to enhance the experience of a particular sport and/or program. A student athlete in financial need of meeting any costs is eagerly covered by alumni and/or current parents; such SOS signals are met quickly.

In short, athletics provide a positive glue to bind together many groups in a school community and to build up the spirit. There are innumerable benefits that students gain from their participation in athletics. A school's reputation can also be enhanced by excellent teams. Conversely, shenanigans by athletes can also lead to bad press and tarnish a school's reputation (e.g., a disruptive unsupervised house party by the football team, fights during or after the game, unsportsmanlike conduct, athletes use and/or possession of controlled substances, etc.).

This can help or hinder recruitment for a Catholic school upon which the life of a school depends. Parents will want to choose a school where they feel their sons and daughters are safe and around kids who come from families that share their values. If a school's athletic program has such a bad reputation, real or imagined, that perception will not help. This is where the Athletic Director and coaches have additional values to inculcate.

Catholic schools work hard at forming students in Gospel values, and athletics provide excellent opportunities for students and families to grow on the field, in the pool, on the courts, and at the bowling alley. Perhaps because it is such a widespread project in the school which entails large numbers that the possible problems will increase commensurately. Parents are not attending Math or Spanish class with their students giving them the opportunity to opine on the teacher, the course instruction, evaluation, etc. So, what is not seen is not so easily critiqued.

Those deductive insights will be brought to the Parent-Teacher Conferences based on the student's grades and self-reporting. However, many practices and sporting events are pretty much open and accessible to parents. Many younger students depend upon their parents for transportation, so it makes perfect sense for a parent to be present and better understand the sport and the team. By their nature sporting activities draw many eyes to their work.

Talented grade school athletes are sought and courted by high schools. Successful high school athletes have college scouts in the stands gathering data to offer excellent scholarships. Unbeaten and effective coaches are also in the binoculars of talent scouts for better situations or an advance of responsibility and salary. The local neighborhood newspaper, the big city sports page, social media, and online postings all provide multiple lenses on schools and their various teams.

Schools develop reputations as being a men's varsity basketball powerhouse, girl's water polo as undefeated state champs for ten years running, etc. This kind of recognition is typically free and most welcome by everyone in the school. Sometimes when a sport dominates the school culture it can undermine other important projects in the school.

One Catholic elementary school principal in Los Angeles assumed the leadership at a new school. As one entered the school there were three large display cases bulging with trophies from over several decades. She rightly noted that this projected what the school thought was most important and as soon as you entered this was the message: "Sports is everything here." She set upon reorganizing the cases with the center case displaying materials related to the faith (service projects, Masses, sacrament preparation, canned food drive, etc.).

A second case was used to display academic activities and achievements (the school play, the Middle School Honor Roll, the Science Fair, etc.). The third case continued the long tradition of highlighting athletic awards. This seemed like a wonderful step forward that King Solomon might have envisioned. Curiously, there are many websites with advice on what institutions and individuals can do to recycle old and forgotten sporting trophies and related paraphernalia like the 1962 7th Grade Catholic League, Second Place Trophy at St. Veronica's that's covered in dust.

This principal broadened the focus and attention of the public on what was valued in that school, and it was well-received. Sometimes this is not an easy transition, especially when sports are involved, as current families and alumni have very strong views related to athletics.

As noted before, having full-time faculty as coaches is a tremendous advantage as they can carry forward the mission and infuse the activities with the ethics of good fair play and a spiritual ethos. It is mutually beneficial for the full-time faculty member and the students to interact outside of the classroom. Invariably, both will reference the positive experience of getting to know one another outside of a class. These relationships will only strengthen the school community.

Part-time coaches also can bring valuable skills to the athletic endeavors of a school. Often, parents and alumni want to be engaged meaningfully beyond writing a check. They can be drawn to a school to offer some genuine skills by coaching a particular sport. Many of these adults may have played higher-division sports in college or even have had experience with the world of professional sports. Their expertise and presence can bring many benefits to the school community. What is essential is that these part-time employees are properly vetted and take part in a meaningful formation program where they are educated about the mission of the school and its values.

This cannot be a "one and done" hoop that everyone jumps through. This kind of mission-driven program might be a tough sell to get off the ground, but if the school's leadership shows their commitment to it, the dividends will be great, and it may just avert many future headaches. Administrators hope that when candidates come forward for such positions they understand the mission of the school and that these coaches want to contribute to the culture of the school. Prospective coaches should know that such a program is mandatory before applying.

Finally, ongoing evaluations will be of great benefit to fully understand what is transpiring in any sport. It is worth repeating that schools should have students do midseason evaluations of the sport and a summative one at the end. The value of mid-season evaluations allows a platform to shower praise and encouragement and to fine-tune any difficulties that might be developing. A final evaluation might address a big problem, but it might have been better handled earlier in the season.

The duties and responsibilities surrounding athletics are vast. High schools are obviously more complex and demand more personnel to make sure that all the boxes are checked to deliver a quality program, but elementary schools also generate sufficient work for the administration to deliver. Ultimately, this brief survey of the landscape of school athletics gives the reader an opportunity to pull back the curtain and consider some of the unseen challenges that schools face. Smart administrators know that athletics are crucial to a vibrant school culture and recognize the value of investing time and energy into a successful program and strengthening those programs that are not. Like all dimensions of a Catholic school, the hiring process is at the heart and soul of a good athletic program.

KEY IDEAS IN CHAPTER 5

- The Importance of Athletics to Student Formation and the Spiritual Life
- Athletics Build School Community
- The Athletic Director's Challenging Role
- Internal Challenges with Transportation of Teams
- Safety and Legal Concerns: Liabilities for Injuries, Concussion Management, Social Media, Hazing, Sexual Harassment, Transgender Athlete Policies, Disabilities, Title IX, Emergency Protocols, Government Regulations
- Part-time Coaches Not Fully Immersed into the Mission
- Hiring Part-time Coaches and the Need for a Formation Program
- Public Relations When Things Go Badly
- Parental Engagement
- Not Letting Athletics Dominate the School
- Importance of Student Evaluations During a Season, Not Just at the End.

NOTES

1. Kelly (2015)
2. Burnett (2020)

Chapter 6

Technology

Its Joys and Woes!

Technology has introduced some amazing innovations into schools, but it is fraught with problems. It would be an interesting study to see the expansion of school handbooks over the years from 2010 to the current day as regards technology. Early in the new century the use of the internet and technology was on the ascendency. As more and more people owned a personal computer and cell phone, these devices began opening amazing opportunities for learning.

After the Y2K Millennium Bug did not cast civilization back to the Neanderthal period as alarmists were warning, more personal computer devices were being developed. Soon, students and teachers were using laptops to take notes in class and to write papers in the word processing programs. Bridging the centuries, the internet itself opened limitless doors of accessing information in a nanosecond. Consider one aspect of the time-honored term paper.

As a student would learn to write a research paper, one would need find a topic. After deciding to write about UFOs and the government's Project Blue Book, the student would head to the library armed with a stack of 3 x 5 cards. He or she would examine all the possible resources available on the topic, noting on each card the citation, so he or she could form a bibliography. This task alone took days to complete and usually meant a trip to the public library.

The internet turned this task into something that could be accomplished in a matter of seconds or minutes and would offer more references than could ever be read or cited. A Google search for Project Blue Book yielded 2,580,000,000 hits in May 2021. But as any English teacher will caution his or her students, these 2,580,000,000 are not all equal in their substance or reliability as anyone with the time and inclination can post something to the World Wide Web.

Access to the information highway was progressing at astonishing speeds. Digital textbooks would become available, and many schools were adopting a One-on-One program, that is, a computer for every student with a hope that some books could be accessed on a computer. Schools and classrooms were being retrofitted to accommodate a greater bandwidth as many students or an entire school might be accessing the internet.

What is the distance from Jerusalem to Bethlehem? What is a quasar? When was the iconic monastery at Mont Saint-Michel constructed? The information is only a click away, just as such questions are regularly settled at the dinner table. In addition to accessing this data, companies began developing digital textbooks.

Digital textbooks seemed like a good idea, but it was met with a variety of conflicting reactions. Proponents thought it would lighten the backpack load by seven pounds; students would always have their books with them, not to mention a less expensive product. However, not every publisher jumped into the digital world, so administrators and faculty had to make choices, and many chose to stick with hard copies. Those digital textbooks did not save much if any money as the price was about the same as a hard copy. Apple was a pioneer with the iPad, and many companies developed amazing apps to enhance curriculum.

Dry lab apps allow students to dissect various animals for biology. Many teachers do not withhold the opportunity to slice up a fetal pig, an alley cat, or a frog in the lab, while introducing the sweet but unusual odor of formaldehyde pervading a corridor; these apps could be supplemental to the overall lesson. Another app had rough animation of Shakespeare's *Macbeth*.

During a presentation to the faculty about various apps, one teacher objected that if students found this cartoon version of *Macbeth*, they would never read the text. However, Shakespeare was not written primarily to be read but to be performed, so perhaps the animated experience got a bit closer to the Bard's intent.

Various participation games were developed in different disciplines. Faculty would produce books as supplemental resources. Instead of a student just reading about a particular geographical point, the subject could be explored in great detail, alone or as a lesson on the screen in the classroom. Students could collaborate more easily on various school projects. So, in many ways, the academic opportunities presented by technology opened promising horizons. However, the expenses involved with reliable technology are considerable.

On their best days, most Catholic schools struggle and scrounge for adequate funding. Technology presents an entirely different demand on funding. There is the challenge to have the proper infrastructure and capacity for computers as well as the hardware itself. Schools also need knowledgeable personnel who will use the equipment, teach faculty how to utilize it, to repair it, to keep software updated, and to replace things when necessary (which comes around sooner than one might wish, or a budget can absorb).

Educators speak about the Digital Divide, which produced no less than 222,000,000 hits when seeking a definition! Students at Stanford described the Digital Divide in this way:

> The idea of the "digital divide" refers to the growing gap between the underprivileged members of society, especially the poor, rural, elderly, and handicapped portion of the population who do not have access to computers or the internet; and the wealthy, middle-class, and young Americans living in urban and suburban areas who have access.[1]

Many Catholic schools could be included in this definition given the expense of technology, but given the current emphasis on competency with STEM (Science, Technology, Engineering, and Math), schools may be left behind if they do not benchmark a certain level of technological proficiency. Since schools reach many of their constituents and potential students through the internet, marketing through the World Wide Web is sine qua non. Technology is here to stay and as it has become an indispensable tool in Catholic schools. However, it has also become the Pandora's Xbox of many troubles and woes.

Principals and Deans are kept very busy thanks to the many shenanigans that are generated through use of technology. There was a time in Catholic schools when students were reminded about the importance of good order and following the rules, lest some misdemeanors get entered into the ledger of one's Permanent Record. Many readers will remember the mystique and warning around the Permanent Record. It seemed that this might be the key document Jesus would consult at one's final judgement.

Students seemed to take this quite seriously, though no one is really sure exactly how permanent the permanent record was; it was probably expunged after a few years after graduation, unless a student did something so horrible that he or she received the ultimate nuclear solution of being expelled; perhaps a school might keep something with a view that the culprit might become a menace to society; the school could point to this event as a fair warning of things to come.

However, that sense of a Permanent Record is more apropos today than ever before because of technology. Students are frequently reminded that photos and things that are written and posted on the internet can potentially be there forever, much like radio waves and television signals coursing through time and space toward undiscovered galaxies with the *Jack Benny Show* or *The Honeymooners*.

Impetuous students will typically post a nasty remark about another student when a young romance has soured. Someone will blow off steam with a digital temper tantrum. A disgruntled faculty member will fire off an email filled with expletives, only to discover that he or she hit the Reply All button. Photos will be manipulated by placing the face of someone on the body of a celebrity or porn star.

Accounts are hacked and X-rated messages or images are sent to the school community under the signature of the principal. Vicious comments get texted and shared. The amount of cyber-bullying that takes place is staggering. These are just a few of the digital problems that schools encounter.

The views and ideas that people will commit to a digital platform are things they would never utter out loud in the presence of another person. Adults as well as students enjoy decanting their rage into an email addressed to an administrator or teacher at the school: "Take that!" While writing such an email may be cheaper than going to therapy, and the sender may be raising an important issue, it could be hard for the recipient to appreciate the point given all the digital poison.

Unless it is a matter of life and death, it is prudent for the sender to wait twenty-four hours before hitting the Send button and to triple-check the recipients. Upon receiving such a nastygram, which may include a considerable amount of ad hominem contempt, the usual initial response is a release of adrenalin and a feeling as though one has been kicked in the stomach while one's eyes open wider than an ophthalmologist's forceps could ever pull them open for a procedure.

There is usually an overwhelming and rash desire to fire back a nuclear warhead to settle the question, but this must be resisted in all prudence and Christian charity. Mahatma Gandhi and Dr. Martin Luther King wisely observed that such actions do not advance understanding but perpetuate the problems when both peace makers observed: "The old law of an eye for an eye leaves everyone blind." A far better approach is to wait at least one week and then to make a phone call to the indignant sender. The conversation typically goes like this:

> Recipient of nastygram (the principal): Hello. Mr. Nestlerode?
> Sender of nastygram: Yes, this is Mr. Nestlerode.
> Recipient in a cheery voice: Good morning! This is Dr. Gonzalez, the principal of St. Theresa.
> Sender sounding like a toothless lion: (dramatic pause) OH! Good morning, Dr. Gonzalez. How are you? (Several pleasantries are exchanged).
> Recipient: Well, I wanted to follow up with the email that you sent last week.

Sender sounding mortified: Oh . . . well . . . I was upset over the school's decision to (fill in the blank).
Recipient: Let me give you some background on the decision . . .

What follows will most likely be a rational and cordial conversation and one that is appreciated by both parties. Administrators and teachers make plenty of mistakes, but they are also in a goldfish bowl where everything they do or say is scrutinized, criticized, and commented upon. The dark side of technology is that it has an easily accessible platform for quick feedback and evaluations and often these evaluations are prompted by a bad spirit.

Is there any human being who has not had the experience of saying something they later wished they had not said or put into an email? Parents through good modeling need to be especially vigilant about their children's use of messaging and email. The internet is also a gateway for dangerous situations where young people can be put at risk.

The news media frequently delivers reports of children who wander into dangerous chat rooms and befriend voracious, sick, adult wolves posing in lamb's clothing. Tragedy has followed too many young people and families who have not given proper vigilance to the use of technology. Comportment and discipline are rarely monitored on the internet until someone runs afoul of a victim. Parents cannot exercise too much vigilance and oversight in this area. Often enough, it is a student victimizing another student.

Students will harass and mock other students or casually post racial slurs. When caught and confronted, the alibis have not changed over the decades: "I was only kidding. I didn't think it was a such a big deal. Everyone is making too big a fuss over this. Who really cares? No one was hurt! I'm sorry." One wonders if the culprit was sorrier that he or she was caught than having true contrition for a vicious violation. Part of growing up is learning to empathize with others and to consider (or attempt to imagine) the unforeseen consequences of one's actions, especially if a particular person or group is on the receiving end of the joke.

In these days that are so charged with attention to racism, the use of derogatory words and stereotypes on the internet can often spell the end of a student's matriculation. No student or family can claim they were never told about the consequences of such postings or chatting on the internet that might come to the light of day. Texting as a preferred form of communication presents its own overflowing can of worms.

Several studies seem to confirm that people prefer to text than to speak on the phone. Ivana Nučec noted some particularly interesting developments in her article, "Why Do People Rather Text than Talk?"[2] Consider the following, for example:

- 4.2+ billion people around the world have the ability to send and receive messages via SMS. This is a drastic increase from the 1 billion mobile subscribers in 2003.
- The number of monthly texts sent has increased by more than 7,700% over the last decade.
- 47% of US smartphone users say they couldn't live without their devices.
- The average user will tap, swipe, or click on their phone over 2,000 times per day.
- Text messages have a 209% higher response rate than phone, email, or Facebook.
- SMS open rates are as high as 98%.

Many people confess that when making a phone call, the caller has prayed that no one would answer the call so that one could simply leave a message and not be drawn into a long exchange of pleasantries and/or an endless or nowhere conversation. Or if the person has a specific question and must call a credit card company or airline with the prospect of being on hold for forty minutes to speak with a representative on the other side of the planet, most people will prefer to tap out a few text messages in a customer service chat room with a live human being.

The average age when a child receives their first cell phone is ten years old. Though there are many useful advantages for a child to have a phone, there are dangers. That phone can be a Trojan Horse of improper communication. Parents and administrators do not overhear the content of a text message going out. Texting facilitates cheating, and despite a school's rule stating that students can have the phone in possession, but cannot use it, youthful ingenuity and nature are as clever, if not more so, than the all-female dinosaurs in *Jurassic Park* to fulfill nature's destiny.

Sadly, the access, use, and addiction to pornography is ubiquitous. Parents must be vigilant about this destructive media with Parental Controls on all digital devices just as schools have established screening filters. Research confirms that early exposure to pornography can, and most likely will, warp a child's view of sexuality for the remainder of his or her life, sowing lifelong seeds of dysfunction. Counselors cite the relationship problems adults face that can be attributed to exposure to pornography and ensuing addictions.

While not breaking the Seal of Confession, priests will tell you that one of the most common sins that is confessed is a dabbling in or an addiction to internet pornography. Psychiatrist and Sister of Mercy, Sister Marysia Weber, notes that this addiction has become prevalent because of Accessibility, Anonymity, and Affordability. She noted: "Experts in addiction disorders describe five successive and interdependent stages through which individuals progress into an addiction to internet pornography: Discovery,

Experimentation, Habit, Compulsivity, Hopelessness."[3] Sr. Marysia also directs parents, clergy, and school leaders to *Reclaim God's Plan for Sexual Health*, an online resource to guide people caught in this growing reality.[4]

Even though the Church finds its moral leadership to be very low and unwelcome at this time, it has an obligation to be vigilant and to teach its truth about this dark and addictive world of pornography. Children are naturally curious about sexuality, so it is more important that parents and schools are providing proper age-appropriate information. Even in the best situations where such catechesis and formation are provided, young people are being bombarded by hedonistic entertainment. But there are other dangers on the internet, and these do not seem to be diminishing.

The Blue Whale Challenge was a mysterious game that seemed to originate in Russia, though there is some debate as to whether this was an urban legend or a social media phenomenon that gained momentum by speculation. It was a daily game where young people were given increasingly harmful tasks, such as staying up for twenty-four hours. The challenges became more intense and dangerous leading to the final challenge of committing suicide. Again, no matter the veracity of the existence of the program, the mere notoriety of it should be a warning to parents and schools about the powers of darkness that are on the internet.

Sister Mary Angela Shaughnessy, a Sister of Charity of Nazareth, has been a guiding light for Catholic school leaders. Sister is a professor and practicing lawyer and has been a resource for countless Catholic school educators. In her column *From the Field: Legal Issues*, she along with Fr. Shayne Duvall noted the following, which seem to target boys given the content:

> I don't know if you have heard, but there is a national push of trying to get our little ones to engage in sinful, hurtful, and destructive behavior. The avenue to do this is via a social media platform called TikTok. Let me share with you the monthly challenges that middle and high schoolers were attempting to perform . . . and some were successful:
>
> August: Sleep in and be late for school
>
> September: Mess up a toilet/vandalize a restroom
>
> October: Smack a teacher/staff member on the backside
>
> November: Kiss your friend's girlfriend at school
>
> December: "Deck the halls and show your b . . . in school halls" (expose your genitalia)

January: Jab a breast

February: Mess up school signs

March: Make a mess in the courtyard or cafeteria

April: Grab some "eggz" (theft/stealing)

May: Ditch Day (don't come to school, but have no excuse and no parental permission)

June: Flip off the front office

July: Spray a neighbor's fence.[5]

Some describe that the final cord of childhood being cut is when young adults are finally paying for their own phone and have adopted their own plan (though some will assert that it is cheaper for everyone to be on a family plan). As long as parents are paying for the phones and their usage, supervision is appropriate and needed. In addition to these kinds of obvious dangers, there are some unintended behaviors that are being tracked with the escalation of technology.

More and more young people are experiencing Social Anxiety or Phobia related to the chronic use of technology and lacking age-appropriate social skills. Here's how the Mayo Clinic describes this phenomenon:

> social anxiety disorder, also called social phobia, everyday interactions cause significant anxiety, fear, self-consciousness, and embarrassment because you fear being scrutinized or judged by others. In social anxiety disorder, fear and anxiety lead to avoidance that can disrupt your life. Severe stress can affect your daily routine, work, school, or other activities. Social anxiety disorder is a chronic mental health condition but learning coping skills in psychotherapy and taking medications can help you gain confidence and improve your ability to interact with others.[6]

This is an area where technology is not contributing to the healthy development of young people. It is an illogical paradox that so many platforms and means of communication have been developed (the cell phone, the fax machine, FaceTime, Zoom, Tik Tok, the computer, etc.) but these are not necessarily improving humanity's capacity for meaningful interactions. Perhaps the 1990 film *Avalon* was a prophetic warning in this area.

Among the many excellent themes in *Avalon*, it showed a large immigrant Jewish family gathering for Thanksgiving dinner over the years in the city of

Baltimore in the 1940–1960s. At beginning of the story, the family is full of life, love, and commotion. As the family grows, battle lines get drawn over petty disagreements, alliances are formed, and others move to the suburbs, then a television set appears. The TV casts a mesmerizing spell over the family members and slowly draws people away from the table to watch whatever was offered. Later, it is placed in the kitchen, curtailing all the boisterous human interaction we saw in the beginning of the film.

Sadly, the film ends with a grandson visiting the patriarch of the family who is now in a nursing home on Thanksgiving Day, watching the parade on his television set, all alone in his room. It is a bittersweet story of a family's disintegration, all transpiring in the warm glow of a television set. This film certainly is a parable for all technology.

As Catholic schools emphasize the humanities, they are well poised to provide a remedy to social awkwardness. During Pope Francis's Pastoral Visit to Greece in 2021, the pontiff observed: "Many people today are constantly using social media but are not themselves very social: they are caught up in themselves, prisoners of the cell phone in their hand" (National Catholic Register 2021). While this was not the first time that this successor of Saint Peter complained about being addicted to one's phone, he himself took a cell phone call during a papal audience on August 21, 2021, sending pundits into dizzying mazes of speculation on the nature of the call. (Maybe he was just ordering a pizza for *pranzo* from Bruna's Ristorante. Who knows?)

As noted earlier in the chapter, it is not a question for Catholic schools as to whether they will employ technology, but how they will manage it. School handbooks will continue to expand their sections on the proper use of technology and the infractions and lines crossed that students will stumble upon. While safety will always be paramount, respect will also animate a school's use of technology. Schools are faced with many decisions on the kinds of technology they will use.

The proliferation of technology services in schools is vast. School leaders are daily bombarded with companies selling their services and/or products. Databases allow school leaders to keep excellent records on their alumni. These databases have demographic information, photos, connections, relatives, memories, correspondence, giving records, etc. These provide a school with the capacity to keep classes informed about their classmates with marriages, births, and deaths.

Other useful tools include gradebooks, attendance records, discipline notes, to name a few tools where information on the student is also logged. Does the student live with both parents or one? Does the student have special accommodations? Are there critical health issues where the school needs to exercise vigilance? School leaders are able to grant access to only the appropriate parties so that good care can be extended to each student. When faculty members meet with parents and guardians, progress reports are generated. In fact, these reports can be generated for students and parents at any point along the academic road to check progress.

As technology develops schools will find more avenues for utilizing it and preparing students for the world in which they will live and work. Catholic schools have a unique opportunity to infuse such learning with the wisdom of the Church and its moral and ethical teachings. These lessons can be followed or ignored to the peril of the users. Safety, respect, honesty, and integrity will continue to be the standards and guides. Schools can especially be helpful to parents in setting parameters around the use of technology and its possibilities.

KEY IDEAS IN CHAPTER 6

- Technology's Innovations for Catholic Schools
- The Expense of Technology and Its Challenges for Modest Budgets
- The Dangers of Email
- Student Misuse of Technology and Discipline
- The Displacement of Person-to-Person Interaction Leads to Social Awkwardness
- Cell Phone Addiction
- Access and Addiction to Pornography

NOTES

1. Accessed May 28, 2021: https://cs.stanford.edu/people/eroberts/cs181/projects/digital-divide/start.html.
2. Nučec, Ivana, n.d.
3. Sister Marysia Weber 2010
4. Reclaim God's Plan for Sexual Health 2022
5. Shaughnessy and Duvall 2022
6. Mayo Clinic, n.d.

Chapter 7

Liturgy and Service Can Moderate Technology

Catholic schools have many offerings in speech and debate, chorus, theater, Model United Nations, etc., all which emphasize social skills; in many ways these kinds of activities are the hallmarks of Catholic education. Many of these courses and activities require students to be front and center and asked to communicate in various forms. Athletics also provide excellent opportunities to put down the phone and pay attention to the game and communicate with the team before, during, and after a sporting event. It must also be said that the spiritual activities of the school provide important formation for students.

On retreats students often participate by providing talks and coordinating small groups. Phones are banned and put away for the day. In the weeks before a retreat, adult leaders are there to help as resources in developing talks and assisting the leaders as they keep activities on track. At the celebration of the Eucharist, students learn how to assist in many ways as they draw near to "full, active, and conscious" participation in the liturgy.

Acolytes should know the responses to the Mass and be able to say them in an audible volume and comprehensible way. Lectors prepare the readings, the psalm responses, and petitions, by practicing these in the church; this can also include the quotidian ten minutes of reading announcements that are printed in the bulletin and posted on the website. This will often provide a first experience of standing in front of a large crowd with all eyes and ears on the presenter.

No doubt, there will be butterflies, but there will also be a great sense of accomplishment and a young person's sense of confidence will grow. Extended family members show up as though it were a wedding or graduation when one of their own is serving, reading, or helping in some way. The family's presence is a confirmation of the importance of the ministry. The Sacrament of Reconciliation deserves special attention.

Over the decades since Vatican II, many have debated the appropriate age for children to make their First Confession; some parishes experimented and placed it after First Communion, though the Church clearly calls for First Reconciliation to precede the reception of First Communion. Remember reaching the Age of Reason? That was typically cited at the age of seven; however today, many would argue that it is not fully attained until sometime in one's forties! Some will argue that a seven-year-old is incapable of sinning; those who support this thesis have never been present on a grade school playground during recess to see some of the mean-spirited monkey business that can take place in tormenting other children or stealing from one another, etc.

While the sins of young children may not have the gravitas of an adult, it must be recognized that this is their world, and it must be asked if society would be better off if people started examining their consciences sooner rather than later. Is society better off that young people form a habit of acknowledging sin and guilt while embracing the teachings of Christ and His Church? When one considers a well-formed conscience that has been examined and comes to the sacrament, many marvelous things happen.

The person, no matter their age, has considered where they have missed the mark as a disciple of Jesus; they are admitting that they need Jesus and are asking for His help. They name these sins to the priest, Christ's representative, who gives encouragement and a penance, and then speaks the words of absolution. Consider how powerful an exchange this is when prompted to speak to another human being about the dark side of one's life. Much like telling a doctor what and where it hurts, the priest can offer healing, help, and consolation to the penitent in the name of Jesus. But all along from First Confession and through life, a positive habit is being formed to admit who one is before God. The penitent is not really telling Him anything He does not already know but asking for His help and forgiveness.

This is a practice that can only pay dividends now and later in life between spouses, in the workplace, and wherever life leads. Most Catholic schools offer this sacrament during the seasons of Advent and Lent in addition to its availability on retreats. Jesuit High Tampa has monthly First Friday Adoration of the Blessed Sacrament and opportunities for Confession. During the 2020–2021 school year the school welcomed twenty-two students who completed their sacraments and some who entered the Church. Such Catholic traditions will not only temper the negative influences of technology but will provide spiritual growth and positive formation.

Elementary schools usually experience a large response to the Sacrament of Reconciliation, but something strange happens in high school. Freshmen and sophomores tend to approach the sacrament in large numbers, but juniors and seniors seem to be in a State of Grace and do not step forward as readily. The exception to this might be on a school retreat. Teachers will have a profound effect on the readiness of students to approach the sacrament. In the elementary grades and with religion classes in high schools, there needs to be ongoing preparation before students are marched to the chapel or church.

A wise faculty member will remind the students of the order of the sacrament so that the student does not obsess about what to say and when to do it, but helps the penitent to be comfortable with the sequence. Spending time with an age-appropriate Examination of Conscience will lead the students to a deeper appreciation for this sacrament. The sacrament can truly be an antidote to the fixation people have with technology. Is it not a peculiar paradox that in an age when people appear on talk shows to disclose some of the most intimate aspects of their lives on national television, the use of the sacrament in many places has diminished?

Pope Francis was right in drawing attention to the addiction people have to their cell phones; he described it as an appendage. One must wonder how much of life is being missed because of obsession with technology. Everywhere, cell phones are held aloft to capture the fireworks spectacular at Disneyland, or of a bishop processing into Mass for Confirmation. Every minute detail of preparation on a wedding day is captured on film.

These are examples of people understandably wanting to capture the event and having the capacity to share it with many others with the press of a button. However, one must ask: Is missing the event while holding one's cell phone up to capture such things really worth it? Another question one has to ask in such circumstances is who really wants to watch these videos that are everywhere and more often than not, tiresome? Such questions are worth discussing with students.

The Incarnation of God becoming a human being in the person of Jesus Christ is a valuable theological lesson to moderate the approach to technology. Prayer and spirituality are the original wireless forms of communication; however, Catholics believe that God desired to communicate His loving plan most fully in the person and teachings of Jesus. Embedded in this teaching is the dignity and value of the human being. Schools do well to set technology aside and prepare young people to interact face to face.

It would be a rare case on *Judge Judy* that involves a young person who is not looking off to the side and is sternly told to look her in the eye. Who has not been in a family gathering in recent years with a group of young people and everyone is on their device of choice and ignoring the people in their group? Some restaurants try to discourage use of phones in their dining rooms. It is a sad sight to see children sitting in such places with grandparents and ignoring these elders in favor of texting or playing a video game. Seated there with the wisdom figures of their family and missing so much family lore in favor of passing nonsense. Parents would be wise to set rules of when and where technology can be accessed.

Schools are very concerned about the social development of young people, but technology is presenting many challenges. If parents are not on the same page with the school about proper use of technology problems will build. One must wonder what kind of society and world is being built with the various iterations of technology addictions to the diminishment of meaningful human interaction. It does not paint a promising future, but again, Catholic schools are well-positioned to counteract this adhesion to a screen 24/7.

Serving as various ministers at the liturgy, drama, music, and the humanities are all useful antidotes to draw people away from their screens. Clubs bring students together around various shared interests. Athletics also provide excellent opportunities to connect with other students and coaches. Another fine opportunity for students to build their social skills is in the realm of service projects.

Almost all Catholic schools require some service learning. Primary students might be asked to design and send greeting cards to the elderly of the parish or to make cards of appreciation for the local police and fire departments. As students get older, they might visit a nursing home and sing for the residents or present a play. All schools sponsor food drives. Teens will typically become more involved with direct interaction with the poor and vulnerable and have service requirements each year with pre-approved sites to volunteer.

Consider some of the innovative ways to carry out the Corporal Works of Mercy which deal with physical and material services to those in need: to feed the hungry, to give drink to the thirsty, to clothe the naked, to give shelter to travelers, to visit the sick, to visit the imprisoned, and to bury the dead. Students participate in food drives and work at soup kitchens. As winter approaches many schools organize clothing drives where students can bring unused clothing to donate to the poor through the St. Vincent DePaul Society or some other charitable organization.

With the escalation of homeless persons many ministries have arisen to serve the indigent, and many of these are staffed and/or operated by the Church or a religious community. In addition to gathering collections of money, students find ways to learn about the needs and complexities of what leads a person into this situation and what are the opportunities to exit from it. While not considering the restrictions imposed by Covid, schools have often sought to visit nursing homes or to have a relationship with institutions near the school or within the parish and thereby attend to the elderly and infirm.

In parishes where children are still permitted to serve Mass during the school day, servers are recruited to assist at funerals. The presence of students at such liturgies offers a family consolation but also draws young people into the grieving process as they witness and assist a family in a dark hour. Some schools have a schola of children who lead the singing at funerals.

An innovative trend that seems to be growing, is that of a St. Joseph of Arimathea Society.

The St. Joseph of Arimathea Society is an organization found in several Catholic high schools. When a homeless person or a person with little or no family dies, a funeral home may call a school and request pallbearers. As St. Joseph of Arimathea offered a family burial site to Mary for Jesus after the crucifixion these students offer immediate, practical, and needed assistance to the grieving. In all these examples, Catholic schools are well-situated to separate students from their various technological devices and interact with other people and especially those who are in need.

In addition to the Corporal Works of Mercy there are the Spiritual Works of Mercy. The Spiritual Works of Mercy include those actions which assist one's neighbor with sometimes intangible or spiritual needs: to instruct the ignorant, to counsel the doubtful, to admonish the sinner, to bear wrongs patiently, to forgive offenses willingly, to comfort the afflicted, to pray for the living and the dead. Catholic schools offer service opportunities around many of these works.

Many schools offer opportunities to serve as tutors in afterschool programs as well as assisting with CCD classes. The entire school cultivates a culture around the teachings of Christ to not be self-centered, self-absorbed, and narcissistic. Developing a prayer life and dispositions that consider others and their feelings all chip away at time on the computer and various devices and help form a responsible independent relationship with technology.

In the coming years, Catholic schools will be challenged to keep up with the ever-expanding uses of technology and find the resources to pay for these tools. But it should always be kept in mind, that these are simply tools and not the substance of education, unless one is in a course related to developing some aspect of computer programming. While the Covid pandemic ushered in the widespread use of virtual classes via Zoom, in-class communication is still the preferable style of education. Perhaps the Incarnation of Jesus is the clearest reminder.

God so loved the world that he sent his Son, not a virtual greeting card. In-person instruction was a great loss during the pandemic and as schools slowly begin to return to normal, those relationships that are forged in school have become even more valued. School leaders and parents are constantly learning about the opportunities provided by technology, but also the many real dangers. Vigilance and scrutiny cannot be overly emphasized to keep young people safe and out of harm's way.

KEY IDEAS IN CHAPTER 7

- The Need to Emphasize Speech, Liturgical Roles, and Service as Remedies for Technology Addictions
- The Value of Retreats
- The Practice of the Sacrament of Reconciliation
- The Spiritual and Corporal Works of Mercy

Chapter 8

Who Is Going to Pay What It Costs?

As the coronavirus leaves a financial disaster in its wake, parishes, dioceses, and religious communities sponsoring schools have had to ask the question, who is going to have the money to sustain these projects? Even in the best of times, parents rarely pay the full cost to educate a child. Pastors are increasingly apprehensive to fund elementary schools especially when some school families do not go to church. In the 2018 pre-Covid period, a retired pastor vented his frustration to the students and faculty at a grade school Mass.

He called out their negligent observance of the Sunday Obligation and stated that he was delighted that the school would be closing because they were lazy Catholics.[1] That story may seem a bit extreme, but it gets at a truth and no doubt strikes a chord with many pastors who would agree but would not be so frank for fear of reprisals and reprimands.

Pastors may be supportive of the idea and mission of a Catholic elementary school, but the escalating costs are causing a large number to doubt their efficacy in passing on the faith or of cultivating a vibrant parish. Too many families seem to be using the schools as an escape hatch from the deplorable conditions of a local government/public school system especially in large urban areas.

In prosperous suburban areas, government education offers an attractive alternative to families. When it comes to selecting a Catholic high school for suburban families, one often hears that a family would rather save that tuition money and use it for university tuition. However, this raises an important philosophical distinction between a parochial school and a private school.

A parish grammar school and diocesan high school are typical examples of parochial schools. As such, they are supported by the local community and/or diocese with an express mission to pass on the faith in addition to the other subjects while preparing students for the next level of education. Catholic private schools usually have a history as being started by a religious community;

as these schools serve in a diocese with the blessing of the bishop but have their own governance structures and funding streams. Private schools do not draw any monies from a parish or diocese.

Since private Catholic schools are not affiliated with a parish, they tend to cultivate good relationships with the priests of an area for help with Masses and Reconciliation Services. Of course, many of these private schools are sponsored by religious communities of men, like the Jesuits or Augustinians, who can provide the sacramental services as needed. However, those private schools conducted or sponsored by women religious will need to get sacramental help. Some private elementary schools will offer sacramental preparation for First Confession, Communion, and Confirmation, but they must be associated with a parish for parish records.

Out of survival and necessity, private schools have a much longer history of fundraising since there were no other funding streams besides tuition, which is usually higher than parish and diocesan schools, and have departments for fundraising initiatives. When one travels in England by means of the Tube, you will often hear the admonition to "Mind the Gap." That gap is the space between the train car and the station platform. Minor to serious injuries are possible if one does not "mind the gap." This is a useful mantra for anyone dealing with Catholic school finances.

If there is a financial shortfall in a parish or diocesan high school, the leadership turns to the pastor or Diocesan School Office to cover the gap; private schools turn to alumni or take steps to minimize the hit by cutting back on programs, salaries, and/or services. Private schools benefit from endowments and the usual 5 percent draw from these nest eggs is almost always used for scholarships and financial aid. This is not to say that either school structure has a better financial plan, but the ever-escalating costs of running a school on tuition and subsidies from the parish, the diocese, and/or other fundraising sources is daunting, and the gap is always widening. Private schools have a longer history of fundraising than the parish or diocesan schools.

Approximately 80 percent of a school's budget goes for salaries and benefits for faculty, staff, and administration. The remainder is for maintenance, operations, water, heating, cooling, cleaning, etc. In every school there is usually a gap between the actual cost to educate a student and what a family is charged. Mercy High School in Omaha has a creative approach to financial aid in the form of Negotiated Tuition.[2] If a family is committed to having their daughter attend the school and cannot afford the posted tuition and fees, they can approach the school's president for a meeting to decide on a reasonable payment plan tailored to the family's situation.

Many parish grammar schools have such an approach where a family might meet with the principal and/or pastor to determine how much they can afford to pay. If the fixed costs of running the school are adequately covered, aid can be offered within reason. All Catholic schools make arrangements and accommodations with families who are not able to pay the full costs, adding to the gap. In this day and age, families would need to provide evidence of their need by completing various forms and supplying requested tax return data.

When schools started asking for such verification, many people took umbrage and balked as though they were not being trusted, as if their word was not sufficient; ". . . how dare representatives of the Church not trust my word?" When in fact they were not always trusted, and their word was not always sufficient as fraudsters were not few.

Any Chief Financial Officer, School Treasurer, or accountant can tell endless stories about scam artists seeking financial aid while the parish or school's donors are subsidizing lake homes, multiple cars, summer vacations, siblings in college, etc. Consider the following anecdote. A bishop received a desperate letter from a mother who was horrified that the high school her son who was a senior attended was not going to let him walk or receive a diploma because of being chronically delinquent in their tuition payments and were leaving with a substantial tuition bill.

The bishop called the woman and heard a sad story about the financial challenges this family was facing. He then called the principal of the school and got a different picture. The principal noted that the parents had left their meeting pulling a new boat. He told the bishop that he would do whatever the bishop requested, but this family had driven the school staff round the twist for four years; while it would be nice to clean up the books and say goodbye to them, where was the justice in that? The stipulation stuck and they came up with the money.

It is good to remember that tuition is not charity. Schools operate because of the revenue that is paid in the form of tuition and gifts. There are salaries, benefits, instructional materials, maintenance, water bills, electricity, etc. Most of the operating budget represents hidden costs that many people do not see, nor does anyone really care about. Those school officials entrusted with collecting tuition have seen it all.

Typically, they bend over backwards to structure payments and plan arrangements for families to meet their obligations. Catholic education is not compulsory, and no one is forced to attend, but it does cost a good deal of money to operate a school and the cooperation of all the stakeholders is essential to its functioning in the black. The Business Office employees have developed great pastoral skills in helping people and being patient with folks who have genuine needs. However, most supporters and friends of Catholic schools would be appalled at the financial scams that some families try to pull while putting their child in the crosshairs of some difficult decisions. One such ploy is sometimes used by a divorced couple.

The couple has divorced, and the child is enrolled in the Catholic school and according to one spouse, he or she is the only one willing to pay the tuition but needing financial aid. Many children come from single parent homes who deserve and receive help with the costs of their education. There is not a problem with the divorce per se, but both parties must produce the required tax information to process the request. However, the spouse who makes the most money is usually the obstreperous party and refuses to cooperate by providing the needed documents. The petitioning parent is heartbroken but can do nothing to persuade the other parent to cooperate.

Typically, a call from the Business Office instructing the parent to come pick up the child or asking where the transcript should be sent is leverage enough to get the needed forms, or more often the case than not, to cover the full tuition, because the combined incomes comfortably cover the costs of the education. So, without the vigilance of financial experts, it would be easy for money to be spent on unworthy recipients. Donors deserve to know and trust that a school is using their generous support with prudence and charity.

Every Catholic school is dependent upon fundraising to close that gap between operating costs and what it can charge for tuition. Students selling candy bars or cookies can be a good experience to teach children lessons of responsibility of supporting their school, but these kinds of contributions do not go very far in moving the needle for staying in the black and balancing the books.

Annual scholarship drives, special campaigns for various projects, regular alumni solicitations, sponsoring a student's tuition are some of the means schools utilize to keep the doors open. Some states offer various kinds of assistance to Catholic schools such as free lunches, textbooks, and transportation. States can provide teaching expertise for learners with special needs, but again this will vary from state to state.

Illinois recently passed a program called Empower Illinois.

> Empower Illinois is the state's largest, most comprehensive scholarship granting organization (SGO). We support schools and school networks in their tax credit scholarship fundraising efforts while assisting students and their families through the scholarship process that can help make their dreams a reality."[3]

Individual and corporate donors make contributions to qualified scholarship granting organizations who then fund a scholarship. In turn, donors are eligible to receive a 75% state tax credit. This works for the philanthropists as well as the families who receive the scholarships.

This program came into effect in 2017 under much scrutiny and opposition from teachers' unions and many politicians who have vowed to sunset this program. It will be interesting to see how it fares. It has truly been a life-preserver to families who have no other options but the government-run public schools. It has also been a great support to many Catholic elementary and secondary schools throughout the state. Nowhere in American society is the wall of separation between Church and State more solid and protected than in government funding going to religious schools.

As mentioned earlier, most states have written into their constitutions what are known as the Blaine Amendments. Recall that these amendments are named for James G. Blaine (1830–1893) who was a member of the United States House of Representatives from Maine; he launched an unsuccessful presidential campaign against Grover Cleveland in 1876. Blaine was obsessed with depriving any educational resources to religious schools, i.e., Catholic schools which were being established to avoid the growing discrimination towards Catholic immigrants who were pouring into the country at this time.

He promoted an amendment to the United States Constitution forbidding any funding to religious schools, but it inevitably failed because education is a responsibility delegated to the states. He became a zealot with this cause as territories in the expanding United States were seeking membership in the Union and he successfully saw these laws enshrined in newly minted state constitutions.

Is it not strange that given the genesis of these amendments, that were blatantly conceived in bigotry and discrimination, they are still defended as sacrosanct in a nation possessed with rooting out every imaginable slight or hint of prejudice? And yet, to many of the poorer communities who could benefit most from a government that would allow funding to follow the backpack of a family's school choice, there is little to no room available. This is particularly astonishing when one reads about the wasteful spending at all government levels.

Consider the annual Congressional Pig Book. "The Congressional Pig Book is CAGW's [Citizens Against Government Waste] annual compilation of the pork-barrel projects in the federal budget. A 'pork' project is a line-item in an appropriations bill that designates tax dollars for a specific purpose in circumvention of established budgetary procedures. To qualify as pork, a project must meet one of seven criteria that were developed in 1991 by CAGW and the Congressional Porkbusters Coalition."[4] It would seem that most people simply yawn and shake their heads at some of the preposterous spending by the government, but if School Choice is brought up, it might as well be a call to arms.

How sad that the United States is revoking the Mexico City Policy, which for years had banned federal aid to foreign countries to fund abortions. The United States is now happy to counsel and fund the termination of life on foreign soil, but not interested in supporting the education of the poor on its shores who would like a choice in what school will serve a family best.

Can there be a greater demonstration of hypocrisy and contempt than that of lawmakers, politicians, and judges who send their own children to private and parochial schools but labor to deny that opportunity to those who cannot afford such an education?

Politicians should see how Catholic schools serve as anchors for the neighborhoods many of them represent. Chicago educational leader Paul Vallas cited the financial monopoly of public schools as the greatest example of systemic racism in the United States in an essay entitled *Institutional Racism in America—The Teachers Union-Dominated Public Education System* (Vallas 2022). This poses an interesting question that one would think elected officials might want to support: Does a Catholic school serve the wider community beyond the formation of its Catholic community?

In 2014 Margaret F. Brinig and Nicole Stelle Garnett published a groundbreaking book, *Lost Classroom, Lost Community: Catholic Schools' Importance in Urban America*. The press release of this book stated: The authors

> demonstrate that Catholic schools are profoundly important not only for the children who receive a proven, high-quality education, but also for the security and stability of the entire urban community with a Catholic school in its midst. Professors Brinig and Garnett find that Catholic school closures trigger increased crime and disorder and decreased social cohesion in the urban neighborhoods where they are located. . . . "Our findings about the importance of Catholic schools in urban neighborhoods builds upon—and is consistent with—decades of previous research attributing Catholic schools' remarkable success as educational institutions to their ability to generate social capital," said Garnett. "Previous research has documented high levels of social capital within the members of a Catholic school's community. We find that these schools apparently generate social capital in their surrounding neighborhoods as well. In other words, Catholic schools are more than important educational institutions. They also are critical community institutions. Our research provides new support for parental choice programs and government policies to enable parents of modest means to select faith-based schools for their children."[5]

This book offers some solid findings on the greater impact of Catholic schools in a community. One might think that the evidence provided would convince competent authorities to take another look at laws that exclude supporting parochial schools as they serve the public good.

John Goodlad and Timothy McMannon addressed *The Public Purpose of Education and Schooling*.[6] In this thoughtful examination they discuss the moral imperative of educating children to prepare them for informed and active participation in a democratic society as well as being able to enter the workforce.

While their perspective is primarily concerned with government schools one must wonder where parochial and private schools fall within that trajectory? Do Catholic schools cultivate active participation in government and society? Do these schools impart the civics lessons needed to serve society? One can think of many other rhetorical questions, but here is the pointed question: Why has the public purpose of education been equated solely with government schools?

This philosophical question becomes especially complicated given the context of the expanding Woke Agenda and how it is infiltrating every institution in the nation and particularly public education. Catholic schools may be one of the last refuges where there is still some modicum of common sense informing the curriculum. The Church repeatedly asserts that parents are the primary educators of their children. Schools exist to amplify those lessons of faith and patriotism that were instilled in the home.

Parents get increasingly disgruntled with the government school curriculum which is sometimes diametrically opposed to Catholic teachings, especially with regard to Catholic anthropology, sexuality, and life issues. It might just be that Catholic schools become beacons for faith and reason, but it will take a financial investment.

If families are not accustomed to paying tuition, this transition may come as sticker shock and possibly invigorate new recruits for changing laws and finding ways to support a family's decision about sending their children to the school that will best serve them, rather than being trapped in a government-prescribed school district.

These school districts are carefully gerrymandered to create a class of schools. In large urban areas, government school districts will also establish Selective Enrollment, or Gifted and Talented schools to assuage the exodus of taxpayers and high-performing students from the city. It is curious that elaborate screening systems have been established to keep certain people in the system and throw others to the low-performing schools.

In New York, former Mayor DeBlasio announced a phasing out of the Gifted and Talented Schools, which coincidently his son attended: "The mayor unveiled a plan to replace the highly selective program, which has become a glaring symbol of segregation in New York City public schools, for incoming students. It will be up to his successor to implement it."[7]

Unfortunately for DeBlasio who finished his term as mayor, and was pushing through this legislation, his successor Eric Adams had vowed in the election to keep the Gifted and Talented schools. So, the challenges will continue in supporting parents and communities in educating their children, but government funding will remain a thorny issue.

It is also prudent to consider that government money always comes with many strings attached. Do Catholic schools really want the intrusions of local school boards and government agencies? These bureaucracies will no doubt manufacture endless reporting and accounting procedures to determine that every penny of government money is used appropriately. What principal has unstructured time for additional red tape?

As mentioned earlier, teachers' contracts include a ministerial or mission clause. As noted earlier, the Supreme Court case of *Hosanna-Tabor Evangelical Lutheran Church and School v. Equal Employment Opportunity Commission* (2012) established that federal discrimination laws do not apply to religious organizations and those they choose to hire as religious leaders. All teachers are considered religious leaders and contracts are written this way. Case law is being tested with a growing number of lawsuits challenging this ruling, though these cases have sided with the *Hosanna-Tabor* ruling. But if Catholic schools are going to accept government monies, they may be signing away their souls and need to overlook public improprieties.

How will Catholic schools maintain their mission around many of the culture wars regarding same-sex marriage, gender reassignment, and adversarial employment law. It is doubtful that any school is looking for a public fight over such issues, but when the issues come to light what will the school want to defend? Its core Catholic mission and beliefs or the popular beliefs of the day? Hence, when some state aid programs do emerge, there are many legal jigs and reels that must be danced around, particularly with the constitutional language.

When a Catholic school does close, it is a not uncommon phenomena that the building gets leased to a Charter school or some private educational enterprise. One must wonder, where were these children when the Catholic school needed students? Pastors who had elementary schools are generally pleased to receive the revenues from the new lease, but that center of activity that a school provides for a parish is sorely missed.

Many people have tried to figure out how to run a publicly funded Charter school while offering religious instruction at the end of the day in a hybrid manner. The crucifixes must come down and statues of the saints are exiled along with any hint or reminder of the Catholic roots of the building. However, there are problems with admissions and even the delivery of the religious curriculum. Do the school leaders translate the specific religious teachings into a bland stew of humanitarian virtues and social justice bromides?

Archbishop Gomez of the Archdiocese of Los Angeles articulated the new cultural religion in his address to the Congress of Catholics and Public Life in Madrid, Spain.[8] As he stated:

> Here is my thesis. I believe the best way for the Church to understand the new social justice movements is to understand them as pseudo-religions, and even replacements and rivals to traditional Christian beliefs. With the breakdown

of the Judeo-Christian worldview and the rise of secularism, political belief systems based on social justice or personal identity have come to fill the space that Christian belief and practice once occupied. Whatever we call these movements—"social justice," "wokeness," "identity politics," "intersectionality," "successor ideology"—they claim to offer what religion provides.

These are the ascending themes and urgencies in government-controlled education, and this includes Charter schools. School leaders would be naive to think that Charters might be a financial solution for delivering a Catholic education as it will be entangled by the new religion and dogmas identified by Archbishop Gomez.

The 2010 documentary film *Waiting for Superman* cited earlier presents several cases of inequity of America's public educational system and the inherent problems of financing private and parochial education by those trying to find an alternative to government schools. The title of the film comes from the reminiscences of an education reformer named Geoffrey Canada. As a little boy he believed that Superman was a real person and absolutely must be working on all imaginable problems of the world including the horrible educational system in which he was trapped.

As he grew older, he sadly realized that there was no Superman beyond the comic books, TV, and films, and that no one was coming to solve the problem. Canada stated: ". . . one of the saddest days of my life was when my mother told me 'Superman' did not exist . . . she thought I was crying because it's like Santa Claus is not real. I was crying because no one was coming with enough power to save us."

Another area that can be very tricky is seeking grants. Unfortunately, many foundations that seek to support educational institutions do not accept applications from sectarian or religious schools. Reading the requirements for grant applications can be a bit disappointing for school officials because there is usually some disqualifier if they even entertain a Catholic educational project. The school must be in a narrow geographical bandwidth or must meet tightly worded metrics. "This foundation will only support Catholic universities operated by a religious order of men named for an execution instrument used by the Romans in the first century, in northwestern Indiana, whose school is named in honor of the Mother of Jesus Christ in the French language."

While this description is a bit extreme and hyperbolic, it illustrates some parameters that donors set while meeting various legal requirements in establishing a foundation. Grants represent hard work that is time consuming and often do not yield good results for the operating budgets. More often than not, they seek to help institutions with innovative programs or sometimes building projects. When Catholic schools are scrambling to survive, the budget and its operating costs present the most pressing needs and foundations are not interested in supporting these efforts. Why?

Foundations are eager to support promising projects that are advancing an educational institution. Baked into their formula is the assumption that a school is stable and viable. Foundations do not want to bail water out of a sinking ship; they would view such a situation as a waste of precious resources. If the alumni and stakeholders are not sufficiently investing in the project, why on earth would a foundation composed of strangers want to take a chance on sustaining a school for one more year? However, from the school's point of view, meeting the escalating costs is exactly what is needed most and may be for some schools the difference between continuing to run the school and closing it. This is especially taxing for elementary school principals.

There is a big divide in responsibilities between elementary principals and secondary principals in Catholic schools. Many secondary schools have moved to a Principal/President model. In such a model, the principal is responsible for the internal working of the school, hiring of faculty, scheduling, discipline, extracurriculars, parent complaints, deciding snow days, or Zoom days, etc. The president, while responsible as the CEO of the school, hires the principal, and for the most part charts the strategic planning, handles external relations, and is responsible for fundraising.

High schools have the advantage of hiring a Director of Development who works with alumni, communications, and raising the additional dollars to fill the gap between actual costs and what is charged, as well as finding funds for special projects. Most elementary schools lack these kinds of roles, and the duties of the president and director of fundraising have been folded into the role of an elementary principal; some elementary principals are fortunate to have an assistant principal to divide various responsibilities, but generally, the buck for everything stops on the principal's desk.

Meanwhile, Catholic secondary schools have grown sophisticated fundraising departments, and if they have not, they had better get started. Many schools have adopted yearly fundraising strategies. Perhaps the most common and ubiquitous program is the Annual Fund. An Annual Fund seeks direct contributions from alumni and friends and is usually conducted in the fall of each school year. Many schools will send out an electronic solicitation and/or letter from the president or principal. In the letter, a few highlights of the school's success will be highlighted in addition to describing the needs and making the request. With the advent of many sophisticated software programs that keep track of donors and their contributions, even mass mailings can be tailored to individuals.

One example of the advanced style of an Annual Letter might note that last year the donor contributed $100.00 while asking the person to consider increasing their gift to $150.00. Depending upon the number of letters being sent, the president or principal might add a handwritten note on a letter. It is a wise practice for someone with a good knowledge of the donor base to look through each of those outgoing letters to make sure the names are correct.

"Elizabeth" does not go by "Liz" and imagine how such an address would land. That donor would lament: "Why should I give? They can't even get my name right?" Or perhaps even more precarious than a wrong name is to send a solicitation to a deceased alumnus; this can innocently happen without any malice on the part of the school but developing and maintaining accurate records is pivotal to any school's success, and it is time consuming.

Developing this accurate database is no simple task for a school and it cannot simply be delegated to an administrative assistant. If communications in a school network are healthy, friends and alumni will keep the administration informed about recent deaths, but it is beneficial to have a staff member looking for data beyond the school community. Data must be updated constantly. Who is divorced? Who just got married? Who recently had a baby? Who is in hospice? Getting these kinds of things correct may not dramatically move the needle of a donation towards a large gift, but correct information provides the baseline for generosity.

Bad information leaves a sour taste in the mouth of donors and that is a disastrous way to begin any relationship, let alone one where the school is hat in hand asking for a gift. Many nuns and priests receive emails with the salutation: "Hi RSM! It's been a while since we spoke . . ." "Dear OP, when can we get together again to talk about . . ." No doubt lay folks receive these computer-generated phishing scams by rudely using a person's last name. However, schools need many strategies to find needed dollars.

Tuition assistance is among the most popularly supported appeals for help because donors prefer to see their dollars making a direct impact on students. Some schools will identify the student's first name to the donor through thank you letters, and Christmas greetings sent by the student to their patron; this is enormously effective on many levels. First, it teaches each student the importance of expressing their gratitude for the generosity of a benefactor.

Second, it demystifies the reality of revenue streams, and that the money does not fall out of the sky or that the Pope sent over a big fat check from the Vatican Bank. In that letter, the student usually tells a few things about who they are along with an update on their academic and extracurricular activities; ideally this is done at Christmas and near the end of the school year. Donors love receiving these letters because it personalizes their generous contributions. Some schools will host a reception in the Spring of the year to thank the donors and give them the opportunity to meet the students they have been supporting.

Various people complain that this reception singles out the needy students and can be embarrassing to them. There is not a more compelling argument for the receptions than the contagious goodwill that is cultivated. Benefactors are delighted to meet their students and their commitment to the Tuition Assistance Program is not only solidified, but the donors become ardent apostles for the program.

During the reception, a couple of seniors are selected to give brief testimonials and words of thanks on behalf of all the recipients. In their talks they reflect upon not only their academic accomplishments and the spiritual formation they experienced but share their future and what college they will be attending. Having donors meet the students they are helping can be one of the most powerful strategies in fundraising.

Since most schools do not charge the full cost of tuition it can be appropriate to ask families who are able to pay the full cost and make up the gap with a Parent Commitment gift. Some families might be asked to stretch even that gift by providing additional funding to cover another family who might just barely meet the asking cost of tuition without asking for financial aid. This kind of program takes a great deal of education and promotion in the community, but it engages those families who are currently members of the school community. Development personnel need to think of every imaginable program to avoid leaving any potential money on the table.

Another program with growing popularity is that of Donor Advised Funds (DAF). Such a program allows a donor to combine the most favorable tax benefits with the flexibility of supporting a particular school. For alumni and friends of a school who are going to be long-term supporters of the project, this can be an excellent way to assist a school over one's lifetime to meet the goals a family or donor might have.

Alumni enjoy getting together and reminiscing about their experiences at a school. While 5-, 10-, 15-, 20-, and 25-year reunions are predictable, there are other bonds to explore that might provide support for a school. A Law Society can gather alumni who have entered the legal profession and provide them with a means to network beyond their year of graduation. A Business Society that welcomes alumni who have gone into various fields is another excellent means to bring people together.

African American alumni appreciate gathering and supporting prospective students as do Latino alumni. Many schools have a Women's Society or a Father's Club. Usually, these organizations have officers and annual programming such as an Annual Law Luncheon or Women's Society Boutique. The school can find many ways to enlist the help of these groups to help with many projects and initiatives that are not typically in the operating budget.

Among other possible ways to solicit funds, some schools welcome Charitable Gift Annuities. Cash or property can be donated to a school and over the years the school would return fixed payments back to the donor over their lifetime. The benefactor can take tax deductions with this strategy. There are many kinds of possible annuity programs, and these require real skills of professionals to help organize them.

Bequests in a will or trust are always welcome. Some schools have included a tag line on their stationery asking to be remembered in the recipient's will. Some donors will inform a school that it is in their will and somewhere down the line, the school will reap a significant gift in the form of money or perhaps property. There are donors who will remind the school that the school is in their will, so, for the time being, to please call off the dogs who are hounding them for every imaginable fundraising effort.

Capital gifts seem to have become elusive in recent years. Donors are more interested in direct help to students rather than brick and mortar projects despite sometimes having the capacity to help with such endeavors. A campus or school building takes a tremendous amount of money to maintain and to improve. Schools are always in competition with some other school and are inevitably being compared to others.

Facilities need to be structurally sound, attractive, and offer a wide variety of opportunities for students. An elementary or secondary school may be staffed with the most distinguished faculty or coaches, but if the place is falling apart, families will go elsewhere. The lifespan of a commercial building like a school is fifty to sixty years and it will need major renovations and replacement of infrastructure.

Too many Catholic schools start cutting back on cleaning or adding to the Deferred Maintenance Plan (if there is one) as they shift into survival mode. This kind of kicking the can down the road to next year's budget may be a harbinger alerting the leadership that the school may have to close. Sadly, when a school does announce a closing due to a deficit, families will likely want to roll up their sleeves in a last-ditch effort to keep the place going. Unfortunately, this is too little, too late. While students and people matter, so do buildings, and donors need to see compelling cases as they arise.

For people who are seventy and a half and older, they may consider making an IRA charitable rollover contribution. This can help some folks reduce their taxable income while helping a school. Commemorative gifts are also a helpful source of unanticipated income. People are able to make memorial gifts in honor of people on various occasions. For example, one sees these regularly in obituaries: "Please, no flowers. Make contributions to St. Michael Elementary School." Couples celebrating an anniversary can request that instead of gifts to please contribute to a particular cause or charity, and often that can be a school. People need to learn about these various ways of supporting the schools.

Almost all private secondary schools have endowments; diocesan schools may operate within different parameters. The endowment is the nest egg of a school and will usually be restricted to supporting tuition assistance with a 5 percent draw each year. With board approval, a school might borrow from the endowment for a project, but it is clearly stated that this is a loan and must be replaced. Schools will have investment committees to assist with and direct the school's portfolio. It is chiefly through the portfolio that the endowment is configured and generates money. Donors can give directly to the endowment but that is usually not very popular. Giving trends today want to see quick results and the impact of a gift.

Daughter of Charity Sister Irene Kraus is credited with a famous statement about institutions and financing: "*No margin, no mission.*"[9] As Director of the large network of hospitals affiliated with the Daughters of Charity, she noted that it would take more than good will, generous sisters, and lay people to properly operate their services; it takes a good deal of money. This observation has applications for many nonprofit institutions and Catholic schools. Her point was that you need some margin in the black or cushion of fiscal health to deliver a quality product.

Some administrators describe not having that margin as "being in chronic survival mode; swimming upstream; pretending the school is not on hospice." Such prevailing school cultures have their communities on pins and needles, and it is terribly distracting to the project at hand, i.e., delivering a quality education. Not only is this a difficult parade to lead for school leaders who describe their schools in such a way, it is not going to attract new recruits or seem appealing to capable men and women.

Who wants to be captain of the *Titanic*? Who wants to be the last principal of a failed school, even though it is not solely the result of one person's leadership? These are tough but real questions and at their root is the elusive adequate funding. Maybe the post–World War II Church in the United States became too accustomed to having a quality product that was handed to them on a silver platter by women religious and orders of men; however, as noted before, those days are over.

There are tremendous headwinds battering the Church in this first quarter of the new century. No Catholic school has closed because of anything that was not related to finances. Too few students, meant a precipitous drop in tuition. If a parish was on the skids because of demographics and people moving out, the school probably got shuttered before the church. It takes money to operate a school and a margin of comfort to expand and do creative things. Schools are no longer classrooms with a chalkboard, teacher, and textbooks. The cost of technology and its infrastructure alone can send school leaders into apoplexy. But what are the alternatives to the use of technology and its pervasive appeal, a return to the Big Chief tablets?

Along with the escalating costs related to technology, one finds salaries and benefits (80 percent of the budget) and maintenance increasing year to year; they are not frozen or being reduced. Sr. Irene was a wise administrator and prophet not only for her hospital network but for other Catholic works that have survived by just barely keeping their noses above the turbulent waters. It is a concerning picture to look at the Catholic landscape in the United States.

In October 2021 the Archdiocese of Cincinnati announced that it would be closing 70 percent of its 211 parishes.[10] This dramatic number frames what has been transpiring across the country in every diocese, i.e., the need to consolidate and close institutions. So many of these church facilities have been repurposed, sold, and/or torn down. It is a bitter and painful process. Who could imagine any sane bishop waking up one morning thinking, ". . . what a jolly experience this is going to be?"

Unfortunately diminishing congregations are composed of nonpracticing Catholics, people who have renounced their Catholic affiliation, smaller families, and fewer baptisms. There is no longer a need for all these institutions and there is no plausible turnaround imaginable, short of divine intervention, to alter the trajectory. The real estate offices of every diocese have plenty of properties to sell. The driving narrative behind these developments is the lack of people to serve and certainly diminishing funding streams. If this sounds bleak, it is because it is. However, it is a time to also look with gratitude to the heroic actions on the part of some.

Nowhere in the scriptures will you find a mandate for Catholic schools. However, you will find a command from Jesus to "Go and make disciples of all nations, baptizing them in the name of the Father, and of the Son, and of the Holy Spirit, teaching them to observe all that I have commanded you. And behold, I am with you always until the end of the age" (Matthew 28: 19–20).

A period of the Church's history in the United States found Catholic schools to be the most effective way of carrying out that command and infusing the curriculum and culture with the faith. The Church finds itself in a period of tremendous change and diminishment, but it is not the end. St. Ignatius Loyola warns that despair is never from God because it clouds the theological virtue of Hope. Ignatius also cited gratitude among the highest of the virtues.

Knowing some of the financial challenges that schools are facing should cultivate a profound sense of gratitude for the men and women who labor to keep these schools in good health, which is another way of saying that these leaders are attentive to the financial health. It is an arduous task, and it is dependent upon a large network of supporters who believe in the work. No one person will be able to do this alone. One charismatic school leader once told his high school community about the prospect of building a new performing arts center. It was going to be a state-of-the-art facility and he had all the money it would take to complete the project, but there was one problem: all the money was in their pockets and bank accounts!

Meanwhile, the Diocese of Wichita in the state of Kansas has enjoyed a stellar reputation for keeping tuition low and promoting a desk in every Catholic school for any Catholic child and family that wants to be there. As one frustrated pastor in another diocese was heard to lament: "Everyone talks about the Wichita Plan. Everyone wants to study the Wichita Plan. Everyone wants to replicate the Wichita Plan, but no one has moved beyond talking about it, let alone implementing it." If it is so successful, why has it not been adopted nationwide by every diocese?

Among the many challenges facing Catholic schools, most people would agree that financing the schools is the foundational challenge. Hiring excellent committed faculty and staff, attentive maintenance of facilities, and offering outstanding programs are all linked to funding; all these factors are escalating and will not be requiring less money, only more dollars. Conversely, parents are not eager to see tuition costs rise and for some, schools will simply not be an option, even with tuition assistance. As has been observed by many scholars who watch the Catholic school world, the very poor and very wealthy will likely have access to a Catholic school, but the middle class is being stretched to a point where the sacrifice needed is too great for a family.

KEY IDEAS IN CHAPTER 7

- Pastors Frustrated Supporting Schools for Nonpracticing Catholics
- The Need for Fundraising
- The Increasing Gap Between Actual Costs and What is Charged
- Financial Aid
- Examples of Scams to Not Pay Tuition
- Empower Illinois: A School Choice Initiative
- The Blaine Amendments
- The Public Contribution of Catholic Schools
- Catholic Schools, Charters, and Choice
- Will Government Funds Have Strings Attached to Water Down the Mission?
- Grants and Foundations Often Do Not Welcome Religious Institutions
- Fundraising
- Keeping an Accurate Database
- Tuition Assistance
- The Role of Alumni
- Charitable Gift Annuities, Bequests, Capital Gifts, IRA Charitable Rollovers, Endowments

- "No margin, no mission!"
- Challenges and Hope

NOTES

1. Retired Pastor Expresses Views about School Closing: https://patch.com/illinois/palos/monsignor-verbally-abuses-incarnation-kids-mass-parents.
2. https://www.mercyhigh.org/admissions/financial-assistance.cfm.
3. What is Empower Illinois? 2021.
4. Congressional Pig Book 2021.
5. Alliance for Catholic Education 2014.
6. Goodlad and McMannon 1997.
7. Shapiro 2021.
8. Gomez 2021.
9. Langley 1998.
10. Flynn and Flynn 2021.

Conclusion

This exploration of Catholic schools has only touched on a small number of the challenges leaders are facing in delivering a faith-based education, mainly for children in elementary and secondary schools. Occasionally, there have been references to Catholic higher education because its practices can sometimes create a trickle-down effect into the lower levels of secondary and elementary schools. While there are innumerable strengths in these schools supported by many believers and stakeholders in the project, it will take a tremendous effort to stabilize the schools, not to mention a hope for expansion. Bishops, priests, and parish leaders have their work cut out for them.

Escalating expenses and tuition are primary difficulties which deter many families from selecting a Catholic education, especially if there happens to be a government school of decent quality available. Despite numerous School Choice initiatives across the country to provide options for families, such aid may be too little too late. The priest sociologist Father Andrew Greeley studied Catholic schools in the 1960s and 1970s and published his findings. He often provided great hope during confusing times of diminishment. He was heard to quip once that ". . . the first meaningful state aid check will arrive when the last Catholic school is closing its doors." It is doubtful that any Catholic school with sufficient funds and students has closed.

Spokane Bishop Thomas Daly who is chair of the Bishops' Committee on Catholic Schools recently stated: "We need as many of our kids in Catholic schools as possible, but we have to be honest that we have some Catholic schools that have lost their mission. So, they have to preach the authentic faith—and also resist the idea favored by some younger priests that we should be happy with 'a smaller, purer Church.'"[1] The Bishop described his time at a Catholic high school that ". . . had 'lost its way' to the point where some teachers 'who claimed to be Catholic did everything to undermine the mission.' One of them was even reading tarot cards in class."

One hopes that Bishop Daly's experience is not too pervasive across the nation, but vigilance around the mission and those hired to fulfill it cannot be overemphasized. Too many schools think they are high-minded by hiring an atheist or an angry lapsed Catholic to demonstrate a welcoming inclusive school culture. There is no better formula to chip away at the mission than to hire staff and faculty who could not care less about an authentic and faithful school mission. Only a very foolish mouse builds a nest in the cat's ear.

At one large Catholic elementary school there was a male teacher who taught middle school students. He was a Pied Piper of the kids and seen as a very cool guy. He was quarterback for both sides at the recess scrimmages on the playground. When he attended the weekly school Mass, he stood with his arms folded. He would not pick up the hymnal nor give any evidence of vocalizing the responses. In fact, the statues in the church showed more character and life than this man. Sadly, he never stepped forward to receive Holy Communion.

The priests of the parish noted that many of the students were not coming forward for Communion and tried talking to the man. While his behavior may not have been the cause of these students abstaining from the sacrament, it certainly was not the kind of example young people need. Imagine if the entire faculty and staff displayed such behavior. This is a perfect example of needing to show someone the door. Sadly, too many schools harbor lackluster professionals and it only takes one or two to sour the entire culture.

New administrators often face their own Augean Stable that is in desperate need of cleaning and this work is not for the faint of heart. Many of these problematic people have been comfortably parked at institutions for several years and are likely to have a following. Any move against them can rock the boat and release a storm of acid rain. Using social media, advocate warriors quickly establish platforms to condemn the school and gin up as many people as possible. It is often a strange phenomenon that most of these accusers are hiding behind mysterious handle names because of their cowardice. Perhaps even more amusing is the consistent and predictable scenario with a disgruntled alumnus, parent, or stakeholder.

Many things can upset a school community beyond the termination of a problematic employee and set a community into high gear with manufactured rage. Often when angry people email a Scud missile it will end with a tag line such as "I will never give another penny to this school!" Or "Take me off your mailing list, I will never support this school again." These bridge burning chastisements have many variations, but 99 percent of them typically have one thing in common: The fuming sender has never sent one cent to support the school, or he or she has been missing in fundraising action for decades. Many administrators who check out the records of such cases are given a good laugh, which helps to assuage the acrimony endured—a bit.

The National Catholic Educational Association offers 12 Reasons to Choose a Catholic School:

1. We offer an education that combines Catholic faith and teachings with academic excellence.
2. We partner with parents in the faith formation of their children.
3. We set high standards for student achievement and help them succeed.
4. We provide a balanced academic curriculum that integrates faith, culture, and life.
5. We use technology effectively to enhance education.
6. We instill in students the value of service to others.
7. We teach children respect of self and others.
8. We emphasize moral development and self-discipline.
9. We prepare students to be productive citizens and future leaders.
10. We have a 99 percent high school graduation rate. 85 percent of our graduates go to college.
11. We cultivate a faculty and staff of people who are dedicated, caring and effective.
12. We provide a safe and welcoming environment for all.

If schools and their communities can hold tight to these twelve foundations, Catholic schools have a good chance of surviving and possibly thriving. As cited before, Luke Rosiak describes the downward spiral of government/public schools in *Race to the Bottom: Uncovering the Secret Forces Destroying American Public Education* (2022).[2] He warns about the special interest groups and ideologies that are subverting the focus of literacy, STEM skills, etc., along with squandering astronomical amounts of money.

When Catholic schools begin to flirt with these politically correct and woke notions, it will be no surprise that these will undermine or eclipse the tenets of Catholicism, so parents, pastors, and school leaders should be on high alert. The compassion, kindness, and desire to be a welcoming community, which are hallmarks of discipleship, can easily get highjacked with agenda-driven ideologues.

Catholic schools, in fact all missions of the Church, should have as their common denominator Jesus Christ and the teachings of the Church He founded as these are more than sufficient to address the questions of the day. When these institutions lean into secular agendas, the schools risk losing their souls as many religious institutions of higher education have done. Archbishop Gomez has pointed to the dangers found in the Church when conflating or solely substituting social justice tenets for the deposit of faith. Compromises with the mission may seem small at the time or a one-off, but like the lesson of the slow boiling frog, it may not take long to have completely surrendered the mission of a Catholic institution to secular forces.

On January 25, 2022, the Feast of the Conversion of Saint Paul the Apostle, the Congregation of Catholic Education promulgated a twenty-page

Instruction entitled *The Identity of the Catholic School for a Culture of Dialogue*. The document is divided into three chapters dealing with *Catholic Schools in the Mission of the Church, The Actors Responsible for Promoting and Verifying Catholic Identity, and Some Critical Aspects*.

There are many affirmations on the importance of Catholic schools and words of sincere gratitude for the men and women, lay and religious, who labor in the schools as a positive means of evangelization in addition to providing a sound education. The importance of parents and their choice is highlighted with an admonition that governments should support parents in their choice of schools for their children irrespective of income capacity. Perhaps what is most expansive and clear is the relationship of Catholic schools to the juridical authority of the local bishop.

One must wonder if this relationship is expounded as it is, with the unhappy memory of *Ex Corde Ecclesiae* (1990) in mind. This was the Apostolic Constitution issued by Pope John Paul II to establish an understanding of Catholicism in higher education and particularly in Catholic institutions; it was not warmly received by most institutions, outside of seminaries, and was seen as intrusive or distrustful of the higher education communities. A particular bone of contention was that professors of theology were to seek a mandate from the local ordinary to teach in the name of the Church; many grumbled about this and most usually ignored it. Many bishops did not push on it either.

Some legitimately wondered why other disciplines were not expected to seek a mandate since professors in Political Science, Philosophy, or English, etc., could be sources of mischief undermining the Catholic project. As many new problems are bubbling to the surface with Catholic elementary and secondary schools, Rome is redirecting these to the local ordinary for adjudication. Issues such as flying Pride and/or BLM flags, hiring and firing of teachers, etc., seem to be remanded to the bishop, especially in designating a school as Catholic and/or maintaining its Catholic identity.

In the United States Catholic institutions have a non-profit status, meaning they do not pay property taxes and some other federal, state, or local fees because they are seen as contributing to the public good. This type of organization is known as a 501(c)(3). An institution cannot legitimately take this title of Catholic on its own volition. Typically, it is approved by the local bishop and diocese and then is included on the official rolls and given a Tax-Exempt Number to be used in transactions. Should a bishop withdraw that designation, an institution will be navigating some uncharted rapids and eddies. It is rather clear that Rome is underscoring the dynamics of subsidiarity and not wanting to handle these sticky honeypots.

Despite so many challenges and difficulties that have been identified, it is hard to imagine a better way to evangelize and form youth than in a dynamic Catholic school. It is also hard to imagine a better remedy to so many of the social and cultural problems in the United States than a sound Catholic education. The poor, the prosperous, and everyone in between hears the truth that they are sons and daughters of a loving God and that He has a plan for them not only in this world but the world that endures forever. When this message complements the lessons at home, an ideal relationship has been struck; when this message compensates for poverty in the home life and absentee parenting, it is a noble attempt to support that child.

In 2014 the Center for Applied Research in the Apostolate, CARA, published a study entitled *Do Catholic Schools Matter?*[3] Among the findings and conclusions the scholars noted: "In the broadest view, the long-term benefits of Catholic schools in making Mass attendance more likely and helping ensure young Catholics are confirmed (and remain Catholic as adults), along with the importance these institutions play in fostering Catholic leaders, likely outweigh many of the short-term financial difficulties Catholic schools currently face. The Catholic Church would be weakened significantly by continued losses of Catholic schools."

Saint Peter Canisius is recognized as the great apostle to Germany in the aftermath of the Protestant Reformation. His zeal and catechism recovered a confused Church. On his December 21st Feast, a selection from St. Paul's Second Letter to Timothy (4:1–5) provides the first reading for that day. It provides an excellent charter and guiding star for Catholic school leaders, teachers, parents, alumni, and all stakeholders:

> Beloved: I charge you in the presence of God and of Christ Jesus, who will judge the living and the dead, and by his appearing and his kingly power: proclaim the word; be persistent whether it is convenient or inconvenient; convince, reprimand, encourage through all patience and teaching. For the time will come when people will not tolerate sound doctrine but, following their own desires and insatiable curiosity, will accumulate teachers and will stop listening to the truth and will be diverted to myths. But you, be self-possessed in all circumstances; put up with hardship; perform the work of an evangelist; fulfill your ministry.

NOTES

1. Desmond 2022
2. Rosiak 2022
3. Center for Applied Research in the Apostolate 2014

Bibliography

Alliance for Catholic Education. 2014. "Lost Classroom, Lost Community." June 24. http://ace.nd.edu/news/lost-classroom-lost-community.
Ansberry, Clare. 2021. "Young People Say Disconnect Keeps Them From Church." *Wall Street Journal*, October 25.
Ayers, David. 2021. "Young American Catholics and the Normalization of Lesbian and Gay Sexuality." Crisis Magazine. May 19. Accessed May 20, 2021. https://www.crisismagazine.com/2021/young-american-catholics-and-the-normalization-of-lesbian-and-gay-sexuality.
Burnett, Clay. 2020. Top Ten Safety and Legal Issues in High School Athletics. April 11. Accessed January 25, 2022. https://www.finalforms.com/blog/top-10-safety-and-legal-issues-in-high-school-athletics.
Camera, Lauren. 2019. "Sharp Nationwide Enrollment Drop in Teacher Prep Programs Cause for Alarm." usnews.com. December 3. Accessed January 7, 2022. https://www.usnews.com/news/education-news/articles/2019-12-03/sharp-nationwide-enrollment-drop-in-teacher-prep-programs-cause-for-alarm.
Caruso, Michael. 2012. *When the Sisters Said Farewell: The Transition of Leadership in Catholic Elementary Schools.* Lanham, Maryland: Rowman and Littlefield.
Catholic Higher Education Supporting Catholic Schools (CHESCS). 2021. Accessed October 11, 2022. https://www.ncea.org/NCEA/What_We_Do/Advocacy/Catholic_Higher_Education_Supporting_Catholic_Schools__CHESCS_/NCEA/What_We_Do/Advocacy/Catholic_Higher_Education_Supporting_Catholic_Schools.aspx?hkey=2036a87a-0331-4290-b63e-721c59c61e2b.
Catechesis and Policy on Questions Concerning Gender Theory. January 20. Accessed January 27, 2022. https://www.archmil.org/ArchMil/attachments/2022GenderTheoryfinal.pdf.
Center for Applied Research in the Apostolate. 2014. Do Catholic Schools Matter? https://www.dmdiocese.org/filesimages/Schools/Strategic%20Plan/CARA%20study%20on%20mass%20attendance%20and%20Catholic%20education.pdf
Clare, Elizabeth. 2022. Catholic Homeschool Programs: A Side by Side Comparison. January 15. https://www.elizabethclareblog.com/catholic-homeschool-programs-a-side-by-side-comparison/.

Congressional Pig Book. 2021. November 8. https://www.cagw.org/reporting/pig-book.
Desmond, Joan Frawley. 2022. "Bishop Thomas Daly: 'School Choice Is Coming to America' (Season 3—Ep. 1)." National Catholic Register. March 7. Accessed March 15, 2022. https://www.ncregister.com/audio/religious-freedom-matters-s3e1-bishop-thomas-daly.
Dolan, Jay. 2002. *In Search of an American Catholicism: A History of Religion and Culture in Tension*. Oxford: Oxford University Press.
———. 1985. The American Catholic Experiment. New York: Galilee Books.
Dreher, Rod. 2017. *The Benedict Option: A Strategy for Christians in a Post-Christian Nation*. Sentinel.
Empower Illinois. n.d.
Flynn, Brendan, and JD Flynn. 2021. "The Pillar." What Cincinnati's consolidation plans say about the Church's future. October 14. https://www.pillarcatholic.com/p/what-cincinnatis-consolidation-plans.
Gomez, José H. 2021. "Reflections on the Church and America's New Religions." LA Catholics. November 4. https://archbishopgomez.org/blog/reflections-on-the-church-and-americas-new-religions.
Goodlad, John I., and Timothy J. McMannon. 1997. *The Public Purpose of Education and Schooling*. San Francisco: Jossey-Bass.
Hart, Y. "Blaine Amendment." *In Catholic Schools in the United States: An Encyclopedia*, Vol. 1 (71–72). Westport, CT: Greenwood Press, 2004.
Kellmeyer, Steve. 2005. *Destined to Fail: Catholic Education in America*. Peoria, IL: Bridegroom Press.
Kelly, Patrick. 2015. *Youth Sport and Spirituality: Catholic Perspectives*. South Bend: University of Notre Dame Press.
Kitson, Donald. n.d. *Picturequotes.me*. Accessed October 11, 2022.
Langley, Monica. 1998. "Money Order: Nuns' Zeal for Profits Shapes Hospital Chain, Wins Fans." *Wall Street Journal*. January 7. https://www.wsj.com/articles/SB884125250840147000.
Lipka, Michael. 2014. "Young U.S. Catholics overwhelmingly accepting of homosexuality." Pew Research Center. October 16. Accessed May 20, 2021. https://www.pewresearch.org/fact-tank/2014/10/16/young-u-s-catholics-overwhelmingly-accepting-of-homosexuality/.
Liptak, Dolores. 1989. *Immigrants and Their Church (Bicentennial History of the Catholic Church in America)*. New York. Macmillan Publishing Company.
Mayo Clinic. n.d. "Social anxiety disorder (social phobia)." Mayo Clinic. Accessed May 31, 2021. https://www.mayoclinic.org/diseases-conditions/social-anxiety-disorder/symptoms-causes/syc-20353561.
Mercy High School. n.d. Mercy High School Financial Assistance. Accessed March 20, 2022. https://www.mercyhigh.org/admissions/financial-assistance.cfm.
Moran, G.P. *Sending Out Ireland's Poor: Assisted Emigration to North America in the Nineteenth Century*. Portland, OR: Four Courts Press, 2004.
National Catholic Educational Association. 2021. *DISCOVER AND CELEBRATE #CSW23 Home Page » Planning Tools » A Dozen Reasons to Choose Catholic*

School. Accessed October 11, 2022. https://www.ncea.org/csw/CSW/Planning_Tools/A_Dozen_Reasons_to_Choose_Catholic_Schools.aspx.

National Catholic Register. 2021. "Pope Francis to Youth in Greece: Don't Be 'Prisoners of the Cell Phone.'" National Catholic Register. December 6. Accessed December 6, 2021. https://www.ncregister.com/cna/pope-francis-to-youth-in-greece-don-t-be-prisoners-of-the-cell-phone.

Nucec, Ivana. n.d. "Why Do People Rather Text than Talk." paldesk. Accessed May 29, 2021. https://www.paldesk.com/why-do-people-rather-text-than-talk/.

Olivera, Kate. 2021. Students at Catholic High School in San Francisco Stage Walkout Protest of Pro-Life Assembly. November 3. Accessed November, 2021. https://www.ncregister.com/cna/students-at-catholic-high-school-in-san-francisco-stage-walkout-protest-of-pro-life-assembly.

"One Hundred Years of Catholic Education: Historical Essays in Honor of the Centennial of the National Catholic Educational Association." Edited by John Augenstein, Christopher Kauffman, and Robert Wister. Washington, DC: National Catholic Educational Association.

Perkins Ryan, Mary. 1964. *Are Parochial Schools the Answer? Catholic Education in the Light of the Council.* New York, NY: Holt, Rinehart, and Winston.

Pope Benedict XVI. 2020. "What Will the Church Look Like? Father Joseph Ratzinger (Pope Benedict XVI), in a 1969 radio broadcast." *Ad Orientem.* April 2. Accessed October 11, 2022. https://frjonah.com/2020/04/what-will-the-church-look-like.html.

Quig, A.D. 2020. *Crain's Chicago Business.* January 29. https://www.chicagobusiness.com/education/landmark-deal-catholic-schools-chicago.

RAINN. n.d. Accessed January 25, 2022. https://www.rainn.org.

Ratzinger, Cardinal Joseph. 1969. The Church Will Become Small. Accessed January 19, 2022. https://www.catholiceducation.org/en/religion-and-philosophy/spiritual-life/the-church-will-become-small.html.

Ravitch, Diane. 1988. *The Great School Wars: New York City.* Baltimore: Johns Hopkins University Press.

Reclaim God's Plan for Sexual Health. 2022. https://www.reclaimsexualhealth.com.

Rosiak, Luke. 2022. *Race to the Bottom: Uncovering the Secret Forces Destroying American Public Education.* Broadside Books.

Saint Ignatius College Prep. 2020. July 25. https://www.ignatius.org.

Schneible, Ann. 2022. US Seminaries Grapple with the Issue of Transgender Applicants. January 25. Accessed January 26, 2022. https://www.ncregister.com/news/us-seminaries-grapple-with-the-issue-of-transgender-applicants.

Shapiro, Eliza. 2021. "De Blasio to Phase Out N.Y.C. Gifted and Talented Program." *New York Times.* October 8. https://www.nytimes.com/2021/10/08/nyregion/gifted-talented-nyc-schools.html.

Shaughnessy, Angela, and Shayne Duvall. 2022. "It's 10 PM. Do You Know Where Your Children (Students) Are? Do You Know What They Are Doing?" Momentum, Winter: 34–35.

Shea, James. 2020. *From Christendom to Apostolic Mission.* Bismarck: University of Mary Press.

Smith, Gregory A. 2019. "Just one-third of U.S. Catholics agree with their church that Eucharist is body, blood of Christ." Pew Research Center. August 5. Accessed June 3, 2021. https://www.pewresearch.org/fact-tank/2019/08/05/transubstantiation-eucharist-u-s-catholics/.

Sprows Cummings, Kathleen. 2019. *A Saint of Our Own: How the Quest for a Holy Hero Helped Catholics Become American*. The University of North Carolina Press.

Starr, Kevin. 2016. *Continental Ambitions: Roman Catholics in North America: The Colonial Experience*. San Francisco, CA: Ignatius Press.

Staudt, R. Jared, ed. 2020. *Renewing Catholic Schools: How to Regain a Catholic Vision in a Secular Age*. Washington, DC: The Catholic Education Press.

Swanson, Lorraine. 2018. "Monsignor Verbally Abuses Incarnation Kids At Mass: Parents." The Patch. May 12. Accessed March 29, 2022. https://patch.com/illinois/palos/monsignor-verbally-abuses-incarnation-kids-mass-parents.

Ursuline Academy. n.d. Ursuline Heritage | Ursuline Academy. Accessed November 5, 2021. https://www.uanola.org/about/ursuline-heritage.

Valencia, Emily, interview by Michael Caruso. 2021. *Teachers' Roles in Student Activities* (November 4).

Vallas, Paul, 2022. Institutional Racism in America—The Teachers Union–Dominated Public Education System. Accessed April 18, 2022. https://johnkassnews.com/guest-column-institutional-racism-in-america-the-teachers-union-dominated-public-education-system/.

Weber, RSM, Sister Marysia. 2010. "Internet Pornography: An occasion of sin of our time." Catholic Education Resource Center. March 1. Accessed December 6, 2021. https://www.catholiceducation.org/en/marriage-and-family/sexuality/internet-pornography-an-occasion-of-sin-for-our-time.html.

What is Empower Illinois? 2021. November 7. https://empowerillinois.org/about/.

About the Author

Fr. Caruso has recently served as President of St. Ignatius College Prep in Chicago from 2010 to 2020. Prior to his appointment at Saint Ignatius he was Chair of the Department of Educational Leadership at Loyola Marymount University in Los Angeles, CA and was an Associate Professor of Education with an emphasis in Catholic School Administration. He has written on Catholic school leadership, spirituality in education, and the historic foundations of Catholic education, and has worked extensively in forming Catholic elementary and high school teachers and administrators in the Diocese of Orange and the Archdiocese of Los Angeles, one of the most diverse Catholic school systems in the U.S. He served on the Archdiocese of Chicago School Board and the Board of Trustees at John Carroll University in Cleveland, Ohio. He is currently a member of the Board of Advisors to the Société des Bollandistes headquartered in Belgium. The Bollandists or Bollandist Society are an association of scholars, philologists, and historians who since the early seventeenth century have studied hagiography and the cult of the saints in Christianity.

Fr. Caruso earned his B.A. from Conception Seminary College in Missouri and his M.Div./S.T.B. from St. Mary of the Lake University in Mundelein, IL. He was ordained for the Diocese of Kansas City-St. Joseph in Missouri and later entered the Jesuits. Subsequently, he earned his Doctorate (Ed.D.) from the University of San Francisco at the Institute of Catholic Educational Leadership.

Fr. Caruso taught at both DeSmet Jesuit High School in St. Louis, MO and Regis Jesuit High School in Denver, CO. He was Director of Campus Ministry at Rockhurst Jesuit University in Kansas City, MO. He has published numerous articles on Catholic Education in the United States as well as a book: *When the Sisters Said Farewell: The Transition of Leadership in Catholic Elementary Schools*. He has been a guest on EWTN discussing Catholic schools. In 2017 he delivered the *Tre Ore* reflections for the Seven Last Words of Christ at St. Patrick's Cathedral in New York City. Beginning in the school year of 2021 Fr. Caruso served as an Associate Professor in the School of Education at Saint Louis University.

In 2022 he will become the Vice President of Mission, Planning and Operations at Saint Louis University High School.

www.ingramcontent.com/pod-product-compliance
Lightning Source LLC
Chambersburg PA
CBHW021859230426
43671CB00006B/452